Dedicated to my delightful husband, best friend and arch-nemesis of mundane moments, Rob. He is relentlessly supportive, pretends to be a not-so-soft critic, and makes me a better artist.

Table of Contents

Introduction 6

The Story of Silk 8

Fibers and Supplies 10

Making Silk Fusion 18

Using Silk Fusion. 32

Projects and Patterns 36

Gallery 74

Resources 86

Acknowledgements 87

About the Author 88

BREAKING THROUGH
30 x 20 in.
Silk fusion, Angelina, machine stitched to cotton backing

Introduction

Silk fusion, or fabric made from silk fibers, is a perfect canvas for so many art projects. Whether you're a quilter, mixed media artist, garment creator or crafter, you'll find silk fusion is delicious to work with and include in your creations and designs. Because silk fusion is made from the fibers of silk, it offers a rich, luxurious shine and intense colors while keeping a soft supple touch. You can use it alone or with your favorite fabrics and other textiles. The process of creating silk fusion is filled with wonder and surprises, and the final product is a delight to stitch on. Each piece you make is exciting and original.

You can incorporate silk fusion into your quilts and art quilts. It is the perfect material for fusible and machine applique because cut edges do not fray. It can be quilted, manipulated and molded into bowls and vases. It is strong as steel yet delicate, making it perfect for handmade items such as wallets and purses. It can be washed, so is suitable for garments. The surface can be stenciled, painted with textile paints, stamped, beaded and used in collage, jewelry and book coverings. Silk fusion provides a fantastic drawing surface for inks, oil pastels or acrylic paints.

As an artist, working with a fabric you created yourself from raw silk fibers is incredibly rewarding and satisfying.

RIGHT: *I made this piece, "Poppy," by appliqueing petals made of silk fusion on to a silk fusion background. Each petal was cut and placed separately, then stitched and embellished with beads.*

The silk fibers we use in silk fusion look a lot like wool rovings used in the process of felting. But unlike wool fibers, silk fibers have no protruding scales that cling to each other when agitated with soap and water. Applying readily available textile medium to the silk fibers allows us to fuse them together.

Silk fusion has not been around for long: We began seeing its development after a felter in Holland, Inge Evers, incorporated silk fiber into her wool felt by using wallpaper paste in 1989. Silk fusion is a new artistic medium when compared to such things as paint, clay, fabric and paper, for example. This new medium is exciting to me because I believe that the use of silk fusion is ready to be discovered and used broadly in the world of art.

RICH AND COLORFUL

Silk shimmers because of the triangular prism-like structure of the silk fiber, which allows silk cloth to refract incoming light at different angles and produce different colors. The flat surfaces of the fibers reflect light at many angles, giving silk a natural sheen. When working with the final product of silk fusion, you will notice the colors changing as you rotate your piece around.

I often have students come back to me with their finished piece disappointed that it doesn't "shine" like mine do. When I hold their piece up in the light, it magically comes to life. Is it really magic? No. It is simply the difference between the lighting they viewed the piece with at home and the lighting we view it with in my studio. For this reason, lighting is very important when displaying a finished art piece made with silk fusion (or silk in any permutation) and also when photographing it.

Silk is said to be as strong as steel (of similar size) in tensile strength, and is the strongest natural fiber known to man.

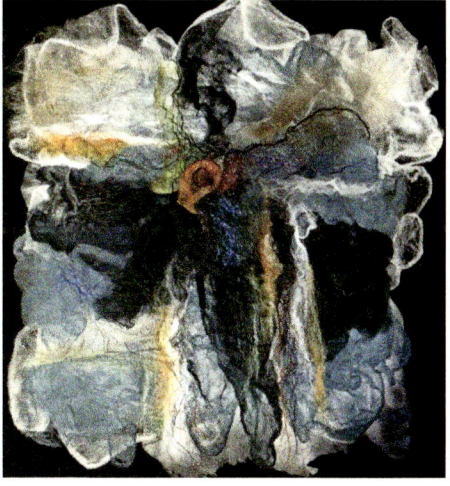

TOP: *Detail of colorful silk fusion made with hand-dyed silk hankies (stretched and flattened silk cocoons).* MIDDLE: *A combination of silk rovings, silk hankies and recycled silk threads come together to create silk fusion with an organic shape.* RIGHT: *Recycled silk threads were combined with silk rovings and hankies in this piece.*

The Story of Silk

Silk is one of the oldest known textile fibers and according to Chinese tradition was used as long ago as the 27th century BC. The silkworm moth was originally a native of China, and for about 30 centuries the gathering and weaving of silk was a secret process, known only to the Chinese.

Silk is an animal-protein fiber produced by certain insects to build their cocoons and webs. Although many insects produce silk, only the filament produced by the "silkworm" is used by the commercial silk industry. Technically, it is not a worm. It is the larva or caterpillar of a moth in the family Bombicidae. There are two major types of silk fiber depending on which species of caterpillar spins the silk. The Bombyx mori are only fed mulberry leaves and produce a stunning pearl-white, highly lustrous silk that is commonly known as mulberry silk. The Chinese Tussah silkworms are reared in the wild on tree leaves, mostly oak, which contain tannin. Tussah silkworms spin a lovely, honey-colored fiber that is slightly coarser and less lustrous, but also less expensive.

THE NITTY GRITTY

Silkworms possess a pair of specially modified salivary glands called sericteries, which produce a fibroin, or liquid silk, and force it through openings in the head called spinnerets. The liquid silk is coated in sericin, a water-soluble protective gum, which solidifies on contact with the air. The industrious caterpillar spins about a mile of filament in just two to three days. Harvested cocoons are then soaked in boiling water to soften the sericin holding the silk fibers together in the cocoon shape.

At this point, the silk is handled in several different ways depending on how it will be used. The cocoon can be stretched into hankies or caps, or it can be carded and combed to produce lush straight roving fibers.

Information on the manufacturing of silk abounds on the internet: I encourage you to take a few moments to investigate this fascinating process. Check You Tube for videos of silk production. (www.bit.ly/1E6SDOn, www.bit.ly/1frzgUx and www.bit.ly/1UUVI8A are good examples.)

Often, as I'm pulling the soft, luxurious fibers through my fingers, I think about how hard those silkworms worked for the silk I am using.

RIGHT: *With their strict diet of mulberry leaves, the Bombyx mori silkworms produce snowy white silk cocoons.*

...... *Note* ......

About a month after silkworms hatch from their eggs, they are ready to begin spinning cocoons. Silk has inherent insulating qualities and is the strongest natural fiber.

Fibers and Supplies

To make silk fusion, you'll need silk fibers, a binding agent and a few other supplies that are readily available at the hardware store. Silk fibers and textile medium can be found online from Treenway Silks (www.treenwaysilks.com). Hand-dyed silk fibers are also available on Etsy (www.etsy.com, search for "silk fibers"). Some local fiber shops sell silk fibers. If your local store doesn't, ask the owner to consider carrying them; most store owners are always looking for new ideas and ways to keep their customers happy.

The cost of silk fibers is somewhat expensive, but remember it is silk. You will need 25-50 grams to create a 12-by-12-inch piece of finished silk fusion. To get started, you will also need fiberglass screening, a paint brush and a plastic drop cloth.

See Resources (page 86) for information on purchasing supplies.

FIBERS

As the name implies, the main fibers used in silk fusion are silk and are known as silk sliver or roving fibers and silk hankies or Mawata. As discussed later in this chapter, you can incorporate other fibers into silk fusion, as well.

TOP & RIGHT: *A rainbow of dyed silk sliver from Treenway Silks is ready to be transformed into silk fusion.*

Silk Sliver or Roving Fibers

To create silk sliver fibers from the raw silk, the somewhat tangled mass of fiber is cut into more manageable lengths of approximately 12 inches. The mass is carded to remove all the short, lackluster fibers and lay the rest parallel. Next, the process of combing continues to remove

short strands and "comb" the remainder parallel, leaving the fiber shimmery and soft. When a sliver is drawn further and given a slight twist, it becomes roving. The two terms, sliver and roving, are often interchanged.

Silk Hankies or Mawata

Individually, silk hankies are gossamer thin and as sheer as a cobweb, but when layered, they give a denser, more textured appearance. Mawata is the Japanese word for "spread out" and refers to the expansion of the cocoon. To make the hankies, cocoons are soaked in warm, soapy water and stretched over a frame that is square (about 10 inches). It is held together by a "selvage," which is the thickest and most luxurious piece of the silk hankie. Several cocoons are stretched over the frame so that each hankie is composed of several layers, each containing the silk fibers of one cocoon. You will probably notice that there is one small patch where the silk is thicker than the rest. This is the cradle, which is the last bit that the silk worm spun. Hankies were originally used as padding inside winter kimonos and other garments, and are often spun into thread and yarn.

TOP AND ABOVE: *Silk hankies accept dye beautifully. I hand-dyed these hankies with Procion fiber-reactive dyes.*

Throwster Silk

Throwster Silk is a waste product from the silk reeling process, which unwinds filaments collectively from a group of cocoons into a single filament. Everything left over is gathered together and considered Throwster. Throwster is made up of noils, the cocoon cradle or innermost part of the cocoon, and very long, lustrous strands of silk filament. Throwster appears as a collection of tangled fibers.

ABOVE: *Soffsilk is created by gathering short mulberry silk fibers into a fluffy cloud. This version, called "ButterSilk," is from BlueBarnFiber (www.bluebarnfiber.etsy.com).*

Soffsilk

Soffsilk is a unique premium-grade, short-staple, hand-dyed mulberry silk cloud made by Camaj Fiber Arts from 100 percent mulberry silk fibers. This luxurious silk cloud is completely different from its cousin, silk waste. Unlike silk waste, silk cloud has absolutely no coarse or thick threads; instead, the silk cloud is machined into a wonderful fluff of soft, malleable silk. Soffsilk is hand-dyed in a variety of vibrant colorways and has a wonderful short-staple fiber. It is smooth and a joy to work with.

Recycled Sari Silk

All forms of recycled sari silk are a byproduct of the silk sari industry. Most wholesalers of silk sari items recommend washing the silk in lukewarm water to check for color-fastness before using them in your final project. The silk ribbon also becomes more soft and supple after washing. If your final project will never be washed, then you can skip this step.

Many scraps from the process are saved and recycled in a variety of forms:

- **Recycled silk fibers or threads.** These may be incorporated into your silk fusion before textile medium is applied. I find these threads are quite vivid in color and intensity and one of the only fibers that show up against the intensity of the main silk fibers.
- **Sari ribbons.** Sari ribbons are quite large and do not adhere well with the textile medium. It's best to use the ribbons as an embellishment that is couched, or sewn on, after silk fusion is completed.
- **Recycled silk yarn made from sari ribbons or silk fibers.** Recycled silk yarn is also best used as embellishment by couching after silk fusion is completed because of its size.

LEFT: *In this piece, recycled silk threads run through the center and provide added texture.* BELOW: *Recycled silk threads glow with rich color.*

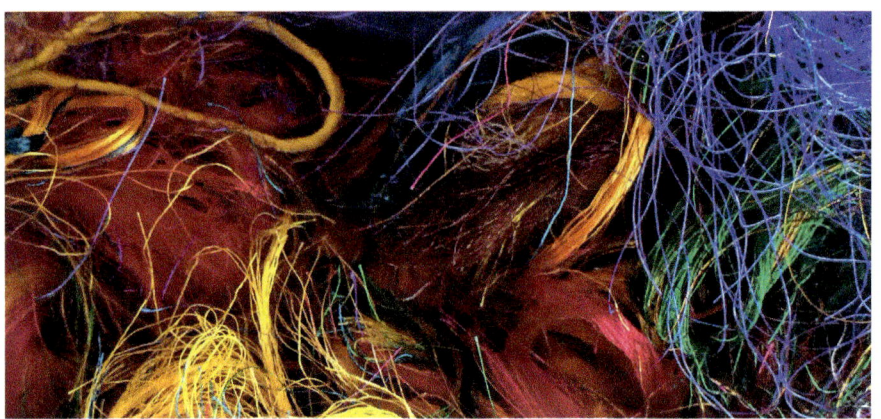

TOP: *Recycled silk yarn is another byproduct of the silk sari industry.* ABOVE: *Silk yarn was couched to the surface of silk fusion for added texture and visual interest.*

Angelina Fiber

Angelina fibers literally glow and sparkle with color. Light reflective, as well as light refractive, Angelina is incredibly luminescent. Usually, the polyester Angelina fibers are used in web form, which I discuss below, but they can be sprinkled on top of the silk fibers as you make your silk fusion. I use Angelina fiber in almost every piece of silk fusion I make.

When they are melted, heat-bondable Angelina fibers form a shimmering web that can be used as fabric or fused to other textiles. To create the web, place a bundle of Angelina fibers between two Teflon pressing sheets or parchment paper and iron on the silk setting for

SILK FUSION

ABOVE: *A mix of Angelina fibers and silk fibers are ready to be fused together with textile medium.* LEFT: *Angelina fibers are sold loose, but form a web when melted, as shown at the top of the photo.* BELOW: *Gold leaf is added to the layers of silk fibers before textile medium is applied.*

about three seconds. The fibers will stick together, forming a shiny, web-like sheet of polyester fabric. Sometimes the color changes quite a bit. Be careful, because high heat will produce a stiff product and if the heat is applied for too long, the iridescence can disappear, producing a matte effect. So start with a low heat and experiment. In this web form, Angelina will not bond to anything but itself, but can be attached to other textiles with fusible web, stitching, or for silk fusion, combined with the silk and textile medium.

Angelina is available in a wide range of colors that can be mixed together to form new colors. A little added to your art mix will result in a sparkling effect.

Gold Leaf, Glitter and Dried Flowers

Add gold leaf and glitter to silk fusion before the textile medium is applied. It adds sparkle when used sparingly, and can accentuate areas that are lifeless. Gold leaf is best used in pieces (a good use for any leftovers you have been saving) sprinkled over the top of the silk or, for a dramatic look, placed in a middle layer with silk over the top but not entirely covering it.

Other Natural Fibers

• *Wool fibers.* These can be used, but they are not as lustrous as silk and are not held together by the textile medium as well as silk fibers.

• *Bamboo fibers.* Bamboo fiber is quite luxurious and can be used along with silk fibers. As with wool, bamboo is not quite as lustrous.

• *Other fibers.* Fibers other than silk that may produce interesting textures and surfaces are hemp tops, ramie tops, flax (linen) tops or mohair tops. Fine open-weave fabrics of various textures and fiber types (such as silk organza) can be used as a middle or back layer to add internal strength to your project.

TEXTILE MEDIUM

There are many textile adhesives/mediums on the market and each has its own special qualities. After much experimentation, I found that the Jo Sonja's Textile Medium works best and allows the natural luster of the silk to shine through. This textile medium creates a waterproof finish that can be hand-washed using a damp soapy cloth or sponge. With this medium, the silk remains flexible, lustrous and easily machine stitched. It can be used for wearable art within reason. I have tried many other textile mediums and always come back to Jo Sonja's because it shows off the silk fibers in the most attractive manner. I avoid matte mediums because they seem to mask the natural luster of the silk.

Acrylic gloss mediums such as Jo Sonja's Varnish or Atelier Acrylic Gloss Medium, both by Chroma Acrylics, are also water-repellent, and have enough stiffness to leave the silk with a crisp but pliable hand that is easily machine stitched. You will notice right away that the varnishes have a strong smell. Because of the fumes, varnishes should be used in a well-ventilated area.

Acrylic medium and textile mediums should not be mixed together.

ABOVE: *The textile medium used in silk fusion should allow the luster of the silk fibers to show through. Jo Sonja's textile medium and gloss varnish retain the silk's rich colors and iridescence.*

I have tried other mediums such as Mod Podge, Liquitex Gel Mediums and others, with little success. They all had a very matte finish, which defeats the purpose of using luscious silk, and they were also difficult to remove from the screen after drying. Of all these other mediums, Mod Podge was the most favorable, and may be used in a pinch, but the finished product is lackluster.

I have used Mod Podge as an additional layer after my initial silk fusion piece has dried using the Jo Sonja's Textile Medium. It does add another layer of stability to the silk fusion and, applied at this stage, some extra shine. However, I find that it also darkens the silk fusion, no matter what the original color of the silk.

FUSIBLE WEB

I use fusible web extensively in my silk fusion artwork, both for mosaic construction and simple applique. Fusible web is a heat-activated adhesive for fabric and is available in a variety of types. Some webs come attached to one piece of paper backing, some have paper on

SILK FUSION

ABOVE: *Misty Fuse fusible web is sold in rolls or sheets and has no backing paper attached. When applied to the back of silk fusion or fabric, the web acts as a glue.*

front and back, and some have no paper. Fusible web comes in a variety of weights and is sold by the yard or in prepackaged lengths.

My favorite fusible web is Misty Fuse. Misty Fuse has no paper, is a very light web and doesn't change the hand of the fabric much. It is also readily available. I find that others on the market, such as Wonder Under, Heat 'n Bond and Steam-A-Seam, contain a thicker web of "glue" that makes the finished piece less flexible and can leave a sticky residue on your sewing machine needle.

In my experience, the fusible webs that come with a paper backing are useful for tracing patterns. Being able to trace is handy, however I find it confusing because the design must be traced in reverse (because the pattern will be on the wrong side of the fabric when applied). The manufacturers have mitigated this problem by adding a second piece of backing paper to the fusible web, creating a sandwich. I still find this confusing and a bit wasteful.

Since Misty Fuse has no paper, I use freezer paper to create patterns. I first apply Misty Fuse to the back of a piece of silk fusion (or fabric) slightly larger than my pattern piece. I then transfer the pattern to the matte side of the freezer paper, cut the shape out and iron it, shiny side down, to the front of my silk fusion (or fabric). I cut the silk fusion or fabric piece following the pattern, then remove the freezer paper. I never have to worry about creating a backwards pattern or wonder what the back or front of my fabric is, and I can easily place the pattern in a specific place on the front of the fabric because I can actually see it.

It is very important to apply your fusible web to the back of each piece of silk fusion (or fabric) before any cutting takes place. As with any kind of fusible applique, you want to ensure that the fusible medium reaches to the very edge of every cut piece. It is virtually impossible to cut a piece of silk fusion (or fabric), then cut the same size of fusible web, and then iron them together perfectly without fusible web peeking out under the edges of the fabric. Cutting the silk fusion or fabric piece after fusible is applied will help ensure applied foreground pieces will adhere and stay adhered to your background fabric.

...... *Tip* ......

To create a 12-by-16-inch sheet of silk fusion with three layers of fibers, you will need approximately 25 grams of fiber.

SUPPLIES AND TOOLS

Fiberglass Screen

The screen I use is the same fiberglass screen used in home window screens. I prefer this type of screen because it's readily available in local hardware stores and it provides a solid structure for wetting the silk and applying the textile medium. I purchase the screen in rolls that are 36 inches wide and 30 feet long, but some hardware stores have scraps left over from repairing window screens that are available at a discount. The screen gets sticky with continued use, so after about three uses, I usually throw my screen away and start with a fresh clean screen.

Tulle

As an alternate to fiberglass screen, tulle can be used. It is a bit easier to pull from the silk fusion when it has fully dried, but I find it a bit more difficult to work with when wetting the silk fusion. The "sandwich" of tulle and silk fibers does not lay firm and flat when a wet brush is pulled across it.

Fine-mesh Nylon

This netting is similar in function to tulle, but is just a bit stiffer.

Brush

I use the cheapest utility brushes from the painting section of the hardware store. They cost about a dollar a piece, or less if you buy the 10 pack. I have used one brush for the last two years. Be sure to rinse the brush in soap and water after each use, and dry with the bristles up to ensure a long life.

Soap and Water

Any liquid soap can be used with this process. I use about a quarter size of dish soap or hand soap per cup of water. Through much experimentation, I've found that the more soap I use, the easier it is to pull the screen from the dried silk fusion. Also, if I use more soap, the screens retain less of the gummy stickiness and I can use them a few more times before having to replace them.

Plastic Drop Cloth and Apron

Making silk fusion can be a somewhat messy process, so you want to protect the surface you work on. Use a large piece of plastic, such as the plastic found in the painting section of the hardware store. My favorite is 6 mil, because it is strong and thick and stands up to all of my wet work. Another affordable and green alternative is to use an old shower curtain. An apron will help protect your clothes.

Drying Rack

Using a drying rack with clothespins is the easiest way to dry your silk fusion. Always place another piece of plastic under the drying rack to protect your floor. However, hanging your silk fusion to dry is not a necessity: I have found that if I remove a bit of the textile medium in the final stages of production, the silk and screen sandwich can be laid out flat. This usually requires a bit more drying time but is also less of a mess and easier to clean up.

Dishcloths or Towels

You will need a few dishcloths or old towels for damp drying as you work and for cleanup afterward. These towels can be machine-washed after use in making silk fusion, but wash them separately from any delicate clothing.

OPPOSITE: *The supplies and tools needed to make silk fusion are fairly basic and easy to find. Before you start, gather a plastic drop cloth, fiberglass screening or tulle, a paint brush, dishcloths, soap, a plastic container and textile medium.*

Making Silk Fusion

The silk fibers we use in silk fusion look a lot like wool rovings used in the process of felting. But unlike wool fibers, silk fibers have no protruding scales that will cling to each other when agitated with soap and water (which is how wool felt is made). By applying readily available textile medium, we are able to fuse the lustrous silk fibers together.

Follow the steps below to start creating your own beautiful pieces of silk art.

1. Prepare your work surface. Cover your work surface with plastic (or any other waterproof membrane; old shower curtains work well). Wear an apron, as the textile medium can stain clothing. Cut two pieces of fiberglass screen (or tulle) and place one piece on top of the plastic.

LEFT: *This is a single piece of silk fusion created with silk fibers on the first two layers and silk hankies gathered or bunched on top to form "flowers." It was machine quilted to add texture, dimension and a bit more color.*

SILK FUSION

The fiberglass screen pieces should be at least two inches larger in each direction than the final desired piece of silk fusion.

2. Layer the silk. First, prepare the silk fibers to be laid on the screen. Pull off (don't cut) a section of fiber, eight to 12 inches long. The silk fibers are long, so hold your hands approximately eight inches apart so the fibers have room to pull apart. If you find you must pull hard, move your hands further apart: Separating a section of silk fibers should feel smooth. The silk should slide through your fingers in what I like to call a zen-like manner. If you prefer, you can then separate this eight- to 12-inch-long section of fibers into three or four workable segments about the diameter of a pencil. Creating these smaller segments is a bit like dividing hair to be braided. After you get used to the process, you may feel comfortable using thicker segments of silk fiber.

Holding the segment of fibers

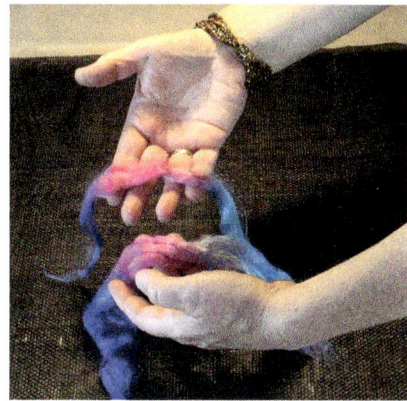

TOP: *Two pieces of fiberglass screen will hold the silk fibers in place.*
MIDDLE: *With your hands about a foot apart, gently tug on the roving until a section pulls away.*
RIGHT: *Separating sections of roving into smaller pencil-width portions is a bit like preparing hair to be braided.*

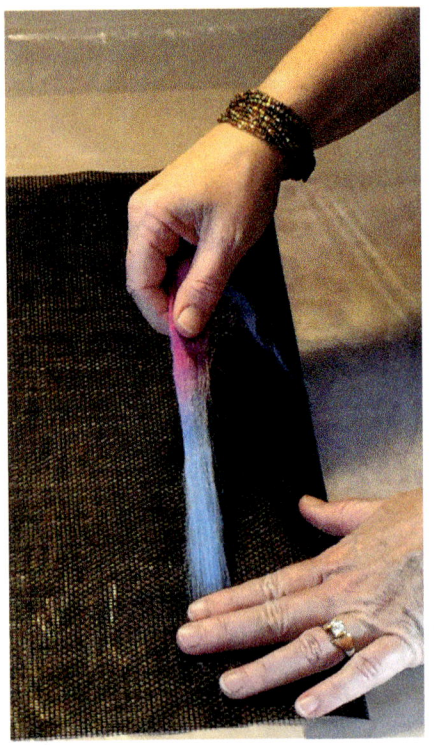 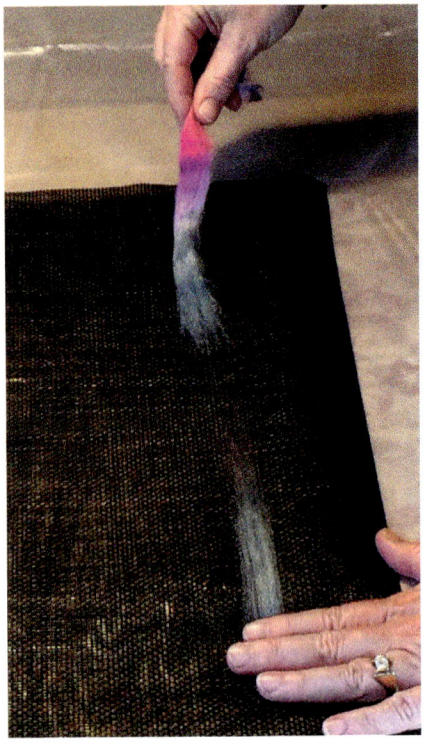

in your right hand, lay one end of the fiber down on the top of the screen at the lower right corner. Use two or three fingers or the palm of your left hand to hold the end of the fibers against the screen, and gently pull the fibers horizontally across the screen. A small wisp of silk fiber will be left on the screen, with the rest of the segment remaining in your hand. Continue this process moving up the screen, slightly overlapping fibers as you go until you have used all the silk fibers in your hand.

The goal is to lay out very thin, even splices of silk. Attempting to work or spread the silk after it is laid on the screen is very frustrating, so try to master the above method. By gently pulling fibers out from under the fingers holding the screen, you are also pulling them straight across the screen. This alignment adds luster and sheen to your final

TOP LEFT: *Hold the ends of the roving section down onto the surface of the screen with one or two fingers.*
TOP RIGHT: *Gently pull the section with your hand, leaving a tuft of silk fiber behind.* MIDDLE: *Continue to layer fibers onto the screen in a column.* LEFT: *As you go along, be sure the fibers are lining up closely together so the screen barely shows under the fibers.*

SILK FUSION

product. The highest possible luster is obtained by keeping the fibers as orderly and parallel to each other as possible.

While laying out your silk fibers, be extremely careful to keep all fibers inside the edges of the fiberglass screen. If any of the wispy ends of the silk fall over the edge of the screen, they will get caught and tangled on the edge, making it hard to remove the piece from the screen. Also, the wispy edges of silk fusion are beautiful, and the only way to obtain and maintain these edges is by staying within the screen. For some reason, keeping away from the edges is a challenge for beginners. Sometimes the only way to learn this hard lesson is to experience it firsthand.

Continue covering the surface with sections of silk fiber by moving up until you reach the top right corner.

Now create a new column of

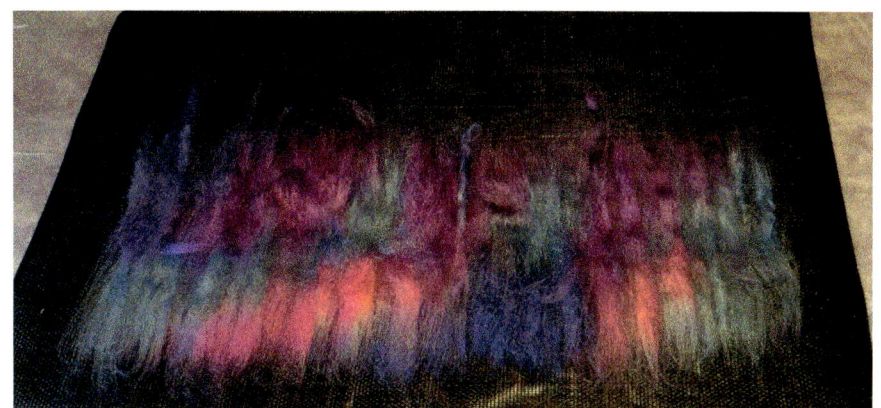

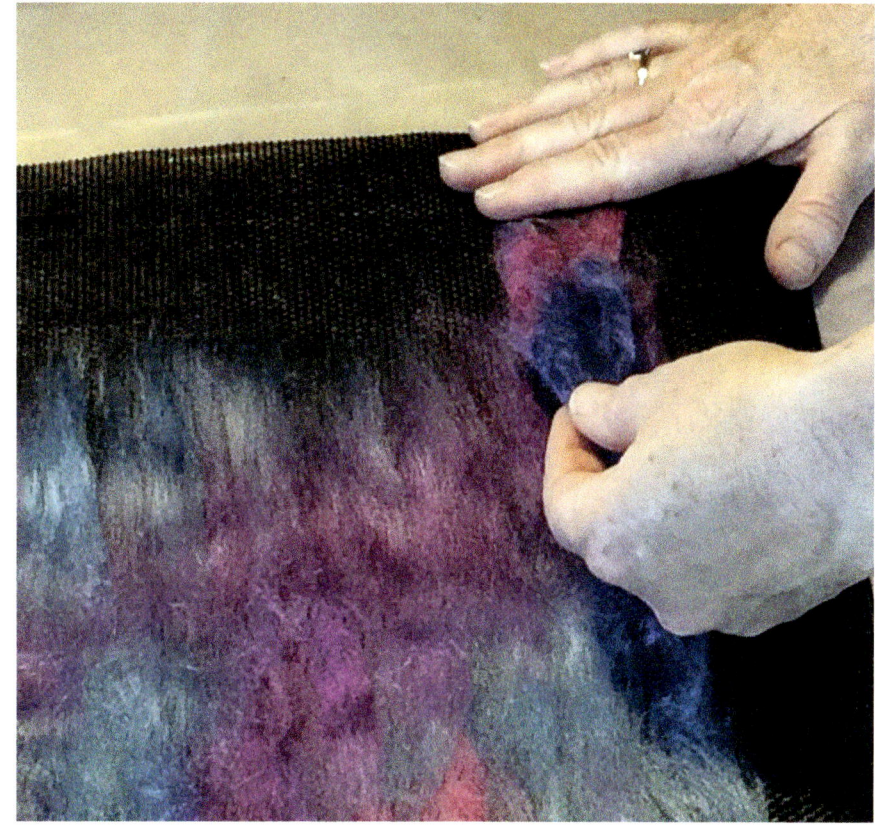

TOP: *To lay the second column of fibers, use the same motion and overlap the first column by about 1½ to 2½ inches.* MIDDLE: *With the second column of fibers completed, the color patterning begins to emerge.* RIGHT: *To lay out the final column of silk fibers, hold the silk to the far edge and pull with the opposite hand so loose ends of the fiber do not drape over the edge of the screen.*

SILK FUSION

TOP: *Begin laying the second layer of silk fibers perpendicular to the direction of the first layer.* ABOVE: *Continue covering the screen in columns and sections as with the first layer.*

TOP: *The second layer is complete. A third or fourth layer can be applied to create a stronger piece for a purse or wearable art.* ABOVE: *Additional fibers are arranged in the center as a design element.*

fiber alongside the first vertical column, overlapping the previous column with 1½ to 2½ inches of wispy fiber. Each segment of silk should overlap its neighbor in all directions until the screen is barely visible beneath the silk. Continue making more columns until you've reached the desired dimensions for your piece.

3. Add layers. Next, lay down the fibers at right angles to the first layer. Cover your entire piece again in the same manner as before, column by column and overlapping previous columns with 1½ to 2½ inches of fiber.

A third and even fourth layer of silk can be applied in the same

SILK FUSION

alternating fashion. If you want your silk fusion to be strong in all directions (for use in wearables for instance) lay down at least three separate layers.

Be careful not to let the long slices of fiber fall from your hand and drag across the first layer of silk when laying subsequent layers of silk fiber. You can gently roll excess silk in your hand as you place it (see photo below). Laying fibers perpendicular to the previous layer adds strength to the piece, but isn't a necessity. Depending on your final design, fibers can be applied at any angle you desire, but your piece will not hold together if all layers are applied in the same direction.

You will find that even when laying down silk fibers in very thin layers, the silk from the bottom layers barely shows through. Keep this in mind as you move toward your final design, as the base layer may not be seen at all after the final layer is placed. For this reason, some people like to use un-dyed silk fibers in the bottom layer since it is a bit less expensive, but in my experience, fully half of the time I prefer the "back" of my silk fusion to the front. This is an example of happy accidents that can't be planned, and wouldn't happen at all if I used un-dyed silk as my first layer.

Keep in mind that any air movement from a fan or wind is your biggest enemy when laying down silk fibers, so keep all fans off and doors and windows closed if at all possible during this step of the process.

Silk fibers are a poor conductor of electricity and thus susceptible to static cling, the most troubling aspect of creating silk fusion. There are several ways to alleviate the static, but none is foolproof. A few squirts of water into the air around your work area with a spray bottle works well. I also keep a fabric softener sheet close by and rub it on my hands and also my shirt and sleeves. It helps if your hands are not overly dry, but freshly applied lotion leaves a dampness on hands that sticks to the silk, so if you do apply lotion, let it dry before handling the silk.

The desired thickness of the fusion will vary from individual to individual. Pieces that will be

ABOVE: *Recycled silk threads and Angelina are set atop layered fibers to create an eye-catching accent in the final piece.* LEFT: *Holding the silk roving in a loose roll in your hand will help keep the roving from dragging along your arranged layers of fibers as you go.*

TOP: *Thickened edges of hankie stack, showing 10 to 20 silk hankies.*
ABOVE: *One gossamer-tihin hankie being pulled from the stack.*
LEFT: *There are about five to 10 hankies in this stack, ready to be separated and used to create silk fusion. See pictures of pieces made using all hankie construction on page 7.*

manipulated or sewn may require at least three layers. However, for my art pieces, two layers seem sufficient.

Once your fibers are layered, you're ready to move on to the next step in the process, or you can add other fibers at this point.

4. Add silk hankies or other fibers. You can use silk hankies alone or in combination with other silk fibers in your piece. The hankies add a different and exciting texture to silk fusion. The thick edges of the hankie have a more intense color and lend a naturally curvaceous element to your work.

Try to use only one hankie at a time when creating your piece. The hankies are layered together and are very thin, except at their edges. To separate one hankie from the bunch, pull from the thicker edge. Separating the hankies can be somewhat difficult, so be patient.

You can place single hankies flat on your screen or on top of the layered silk sliver fibers for an overall effect, or gather them into a flower-like bunch to be placed as a dramatic design element in your piece. Using many hankie-flower bunches together, without any silk sliver fibers as a base, also creates a lovely piece.

...... *Tip* ......

When separating the silk hankies, an iron helps to flatten and organize them back into a tidy square. Also, a bit of talcum powder on your hands will help prevent snagging on rough spots.

 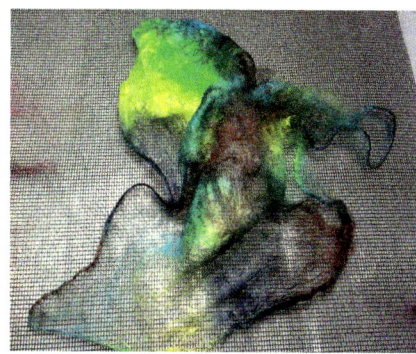 

LEFT: *To make silk fusion from hankies alone, first a single hankie is pulled from the stack.* CENTER: *The single hankie is set down in a free-form shape on the screen.* RIGHT: *Several single hankies are bunched up like a flower and then laid out in a row.*

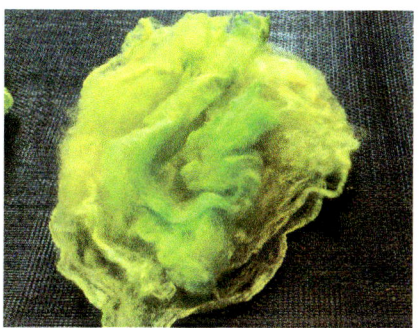  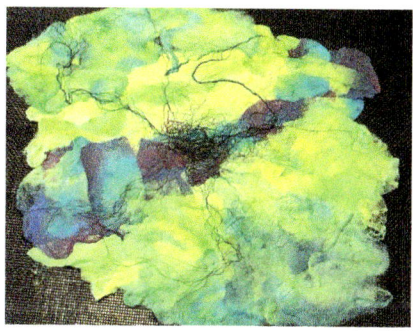

LEFT: *A four-hankie stack is manipulated to create an organic shape. Single layers have been pulled from the outside, but remain joined in the center.* CENTER: *With the flower shapes and manipulated hankie stacks arranged on the screen, the hankies are ready to be covered with a top screen and fused with water and textile medium.* RIGHT: *After wetting, adding textile medium and drying, the all-hankie silk fusion blooms with color and shape.*

If you plan to incorporate other fibers such as Angelina, silk threads, gold leaf, glitter or dried flowers, add them to the top layer or final design as they may become completely obscured if covered by subsequent layers of silk fiber.

5. Make the "sandwich." Once you complete your final design, carefully place the second piece of fiberglass screen

ABOVE: *Once the top screen is laid over the layers of silk, hankies or fibers, the colors barely show through.*

SILK FUSION

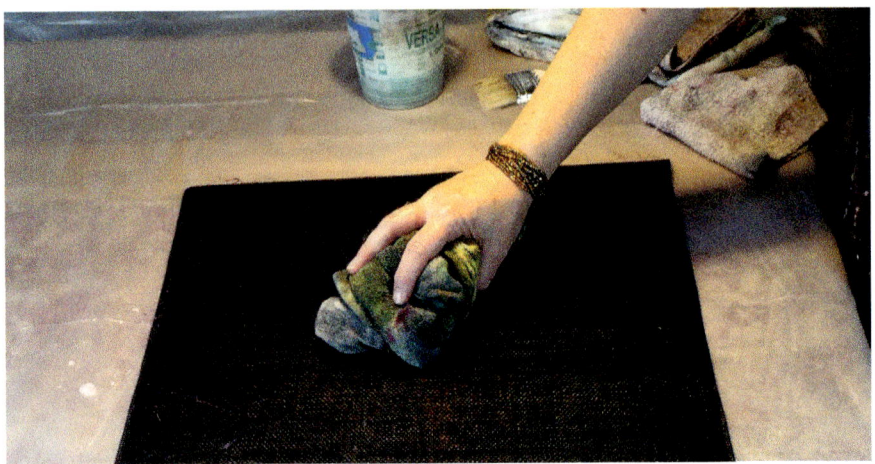

TOP: *Begin wetting the sandwich by pouring a soap and water mixture over the top screen. Plastic beneath the sandwich protects the work surface.*
MIDDLE: *The soapy water mixture is pressed into the silk with a brush. It's critical that all layers of silk are thoroughly wetted in this step.*
ABOVE: *Blotting the screen with a dishcloth can help remove excess moisture, but care should be taken to leave enough water to allow the textile medium to be absorbed.*

over all the silk fibers, creating a sandwich. The top screen will help hold the silk in place while you wet it and apply the adhesive. Be very careful laying the top screen down and don't move it around or lift it up after placing it down, because you risk moving the silk around underneath. Remember, once your silk fusion is dry, the screens will be removed.

6. Wet the silk. You must wet the silk fibers thoroughly so they will accept the textile medium applied in the next step. Silk fiber naturally tends to repel water, so you will add soap to act as a surfactant, helping the fibers accept the water and, later, the textile medium. To create your mixture, add mild soap to warm water with a ratio of approximately one quarter-size dollop of soap to one cup of water. Liquid hand soap or dish soap works fine.

Apply the soap solution to your screen sandwich by brushing it through the screen using a paintbrush. Quite a bit of soapy water is necessary to wet the fibers; I like to pour it directly from the cup onto the screen, then move it around with the paint brush. After the silk is somewhat wet, you can really apply pressure to the screen with the brush without disturbing the fibers. When you think the top is

SILK FUSION

thoroughly wet, turn the silken sandwich over and repeat the wetting process on the other side. It takes more water and time to thoroughly penetrate the fibers than you might anticipate. The screen and silk sandwich changes to a darker color and becomes very flat with no air pockets when the water has soaked through.

Remember, you cannot see the middle layer of silk fibers, so it can be hard to determine when the layers are wet all the way through. Always apply more water/soap solution than seems necessary. You can wipe up excess moisture before moving on to the next step if needed.

Use the pressure of your hands to help the water penetrate by pushing on the screen sandwich. If possible, let the wet sandwich sit for five to 10 minutes allowing the water to continue to soak through all the fibers.

When you are sure that all the fibers are wet, you can blot excess water from the sandwich with a sponge or towel, but don't take off too much water. You want enough water left on the silk sandwich to aid penetration of the textile medium through all layers of the silk in the next step, but not so much that the water dilutes the textile medium. Again, if all layers of the

TOP: *Once your sandwiched layers of screening and silk is thoroughly wet, pour textile medium directly from the container onto the surface of the top screen.* MIDDLE: *Use a paintbrush to move the textile medium around and ensure it penetrates the layers evenly.* ABOVE: *Excess textile medium can be dabbed off using a dishcloth or towel.*

SILK FUSION

ABOVE: *The top screen is removed, revealing the fused fibers. Once the piece is dry, it can be removed from the bottom screen.*

ABOVE: *Push about one inch of loose ends of the fibers together to create a selvage.*

silk fiber are not fully wetted, the adhesive will not penetrate.

Don't be concerned about a little lather from the soap.

7. Apply textile medium. Next, pour some textile medium from the bottle directly on top of the screen and spread it evenly and thoroughly onto the wetted silk with the brush, creating an even, milky look. Again, don't be afraid to apply firm pressure with the brush to encourage the adhesive to move through all layers of silk.

Turn the sandwich over and apply a bit more textile medium to the other side. Work again with the brush. If possible, let this sandwich sit for five to 10 minutes to let the textile medium continue to soak through all the fibers.

Keep in mind that neither the soap nor the textile medium will show when the silk fusion is dry.

Before setting the piece to dry, create a small area of "selvage" by lightly pushing about one inch of loose ends along one side into a thicker edge. This selvage will make it much easier to peel your piece off the screen later.

8. Let dry. The silk fusion sandwich can be laid flat or hung to dry. My favored method for drying silk fusion is to lay it out flat on a piece of plastic. One reason I like this method is that, with a bit of care, you can remove the top layer of fiberglass screen, which sometimes leaves a slight imprint of the grid on the silk fusion. Before leaving the piece to dry and removing the top screen, blot off as much textile medium as possible with a sponge or towel without completely drying the surface. You don't want to remove too much medium, or the fibers won't hold together when they dry, but you also don't want puddles of textile medium pooling on top of your piece. With the excess medium removed, lay your sandwich on top of a surface covered in clean plastic and carefully remove the top fiberglass screen. Remove the screen slowly, being careful to ease any fibers that stick to the top screen back down onto the wet silk fibers and screen beneath.

Although I prefer to remove the top screen before letting my piece dry, sometimes it is just too difficult and the silk won't stay in place as I lift the screen. If you encounter the same difficulty,

> **...... Tip ......**
> After about three uses, throw the screen away and start with a fresh clean screen.

remember that it isn't necessary to remove the top screen. The piece will dry just fine with the top screen left in place. When hanging to dry, I also like to remove just a bit of excess textile medium from the sandwich with a sponge or towel just to cut down on drips. When hanging to dry, do not remove the top screen. Excess textile medium will drip from the sandwich as it hangs, so always place plastic below it. Take this precaution when working outside, too, because the textile medium will stain stone and mulch, and possibly kill grass.

Do not dry your piece in direct sunlight as it is destructive to silk. Drying times vary according to the thickness of the piece and humidity. Drying for eight to 10 hours or overnight is usually enough. Drying flat takes a bit longer.

9. Clean up. Wipe plastic with water to remove any textile medium and rinse brushes with warm, soapy water.

10. Pull silk fusion from the screen. I find that my anticipation to pull my silk fusion from the screen is overwhelming: After leaving it to dry overnight, I'm too excited to even have my coffee before releasing the silk fusion. Freeing a piece from the screen

TOP: *To remove the piece from the bottom screen, slide a finger beneath the silk.* ABOVE: *Push your finger in and down and then pull out toward the edge and away from the center. By pulling away from the center, you are much less likely to tear the fusion at the feathered edge.*

SILK FUSION

is a magic moment.

When the silk fusion is completely dry, slowly peel both screens away one at a time. If the piece is not completely dry, it will be difficult to separate it from the screen and the fiber layers will pull apart. The dried silk fusion is amazingly strong, and you may need to apply quite a bit of pressure to pull it from the screen. This is where the selvage edge you created earlier comes in handy: The thickened edge is much easier to pull from the screen than the wispy edges.

Note: This part of the process becomes harder and harder the more times you use your fiberglass screen because it gets sticky with continued use. After about three uses, I usually throw my screen away and start with a fresh clean screen.

11. Set the adhesive.
Because we use a textile medium to hold the silk fibers together, the piece of silk fusion must be heat-set with an iron on silk setting to finish the bond. Ironing also helps flatten the piece and

TOP LEFT: *The front side of the completed silk fusion piece showing the red accent fibers.* LEFT: *The same piece viewed from the back. Now the silk fusion is ready to be heat-set with an iron.*

remove creases. Always use a Teflon pressing sheet or parchment paper between your ironing surface and the silk fusion and also between the silk fusion and your iron to prevent gumming up the surface of the iron. It is not necessary to heat-set gloss varnish; however, ironing does not harm it.

12. Caring for the fiberglass screen. Wash your screens with warm soapy water and let them drip dry. If the screen becomes wrinkled, it can be ironed flat again. Remember to use a pressing cloth. Also, using ample soap during the wetting stage (described in step 6), will prevent the screen from holding the textile medium and getting too sticky.

No matter how well you clean it, the screen will become sticky and difficult to pull off the silk fusion after repeated use. The number of times it can be used depends on how much soap you use in the wetting stage, how much medium you apply and how well you wash your screens. A set of screens can usually be used three or four times before they need to be replaced. Throw the screen away when it becomes too hard to pull the silk fusion from the screen.

TROUBLESHOOTING

As you make your silk fusion, you may encounter a few challenges. Here are the most common problems and possible solutions:

Fuzzy Surface
- The fusion wasn't completely dry before being peeled off the screen.
- You applied too little textile medium. Brush another layer over your silk fusion and let dry.

Difficulty Removing the Screen
- Remember that silk fusion, when completely dry, is quite strong. Quite a bit of force can be used when removing the screen without ripping or tearing the piece. Work slowly and deliberately.
- You may have problems if you try to remove the screen before the silk fusion is completely dry.
- If the feathery edges of the silk fibers make it hard to cleanly pull the screen away, remember with your next piece to create a "selvage" (described in step 7). To maintain the feathery edges, work your finger under the silk fusion and toward the middle, then pull it outward to release the feathery edges.
- Separation of fibers occurs if they were not thoroughly wetted, which means the water/soap solution and/or textile medium did not penetrate through all the layers. It is very important to wet the fibers completely through, both at the wetting stage and the textile medium application stage. It may help to let the wetted fibers sit for a few minutes before applying the adhesive, and to let the adhesive sit for a few minutes before laying or hanging to dry.

.... *Note* ......

You can also simply lay down the silk fibers on top of a piece of finely woven fabric (like silk organza, quilting cotton or cheesecloth) to create an interesting design. Keep in mind that the resulting softness and sheen of the final product is directly affected by the texture of the underlying fabric. When using a piece of fabric, you may find that you don't need quite as much silk fiber. This process creates a very stable and strong final product.

Using Silk Fusion

Everyone should experience how luscious it feels to stitch on silk fusion, which lends itself so well to quilting and especially art quilting. Here are a few ways you can use silk fusion. I'm sure you can think of many more.

Raw-Edge, Fusible or Machine Applique

Silk fusion is the perfect medium for raw-edge applique, because no fraying occurs on the cut edges. This is one reason it is so wonderful to use in mosaic pieces (see page 37 for more information on mosaics).

RIGHT: *A shimmering pastel purse was created from silk fusion and accented with a braided yarn handle.*

Wallets, Purses and Book Covers

Silk fusion is fantastic to use on the outside of wallets, purses and book covers. It is quite strong and withstands daily wear and tear beautifully. Sometimes

ABOVE: *In this piece, "Goldfish," I appliqued pieces of silk fusion to a background of silk fusion and added stitching to create the design.*

I like to coat my silk fusion with some Mod Podge for extra protection before incorporating into these utilitarian art pieces. However, Mod Podge tends to darken the silk somewhat, and it also stiffens the final product. See the Projects section on page 36 for patterns and more examples.

Mixed Media

Silk fusion can be used just like paper and is the perfect addition to all kinds of mixed media pieces. It can be applied with glue or gel medium along with all

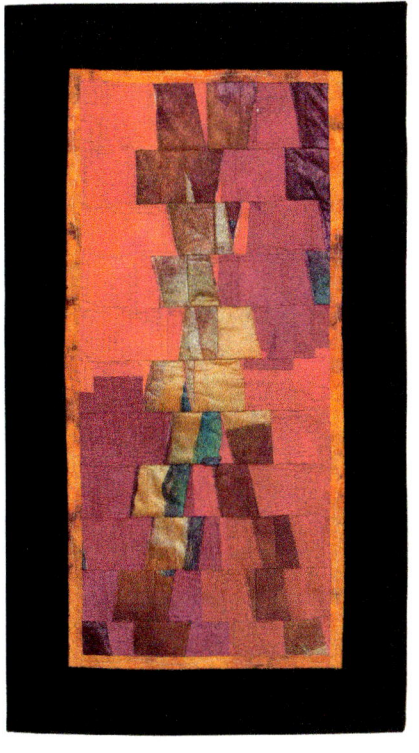

the other embellishments used in mixed media. It also will accept ink and paint.

Pieced in Quilts

I have used silk fusion many times, pieced just like other fabrics, in my quilts. The seams are a bit bulkier where it is used, but it behaves much like other fabrics when pieced. Thinner pieces of silk fusion may be preferable to use for piecing, if they are available.

TOP: *Silk fusion works beautifully when pieced into art quilts. In this three-panel piece, "Bamboo 1," I combined hand-dyed fabric with silk fusion.* LEFT: *To create this piece, "Yellow Tree," I appliquéd silk fusion to pre-quilted, hand-dyed fabric.*

Cards

Be sure to save all the little scraps of silk fusion left over from cutting; especially those feathery edges. For handmade cards, attach scraps to cardstock directly with a fusible web or just a bit of fabric glue (fabric glue remains pliable, unlike regular craft glue). Glue by itself is usually sufficient to hold the silk fusion to the paper, but you can stitch scraps down for added texture and to ensure that the pieces stay on the paper. My scraps usually come from some previous mosaic or applique work, so they usually already have fusible web applied to the back.

Gift Tags

As with greeting cards, you can affix scraps of silk fusion to small pieces of card stock to create tags that will make your gift stand out. Use saved scraps as gift tags.

TOP RIGHT: *Colorful scraps of silk fusion become eye-catching greeting cards, notes and gift tags with a bit of ironing and a few stitches.* RIGHT: *In this piece I appliqued silk fusion onto a background of another piece of silk fusion. Stitching and small beads add additional line and texture.*

TOP: *Silk fusion squares bring rich color to notes and tags made of black card stock.* ABOVE LEFT: *Pieces of silk fusion set in mosaic patterns accent these greeting cards.* MIDDLE RIGHT: *Because it wears beautifully, silk fusion can be used for hard-working items like wallets, purses or pouches.* RIGHT: *From big to small, a journal bound with silk fusion is a joy to use.*

OTHER IDEAS

You are only limited by your imagination! Try using silk fusion to create these items:

- Vessels
- Envelopes
- Eyeglasses cases
- Picture frames
- Matting for photos or artwork
- Jewelry, including pins, earrings, pendants, etc.
- Appliqué for clothing and other projects
- Lamp shades

Projects and Patterns

Making silk fusion is just half the fun: Now it's time to create something with the gorgeous fabric you've made. This section contains project ideas and patterns. My preferred method of pattern-making is to be as general as possible, so the pattern can be used in a variety of ways or sizes. I think this versatility encourages creativity and flexibility. I have included specific measurements where necessary, such as in the gift envelope. My intention is not to frustrate you, but to ignite your imagination.

Mosiacs **37**
Cards and Tags **48**
Gift Envelope **50**
Decorative Boxes. **53**
Sketchbook or Journal . . **56**
Purse. **61**

Mosaics

SUPPLIES
Cutting mat, rotary cutter, straight edge
Scissors
Tweezers
Marker
Iron

MATERIALS
Silk fusion in whatever dimension you choose. Start with three different colors.

Background fabric (I prefer to use black cotton fabric for my background, but any color is fine. Always start with a piece that is larger than your final design to ensure flexibility with mosaic size and finishing methods.)

Tracing paper

Fusible web

One of my favorite things to make with silk fusion is mosaics. Because its cut edges do not fray, silk fusion is the perfect medium for mosaics (and any other fusible applique project).

You may find it traumatic to cut up a beautiful piece of silk fusion. I must admit, the first time I had the courage to do it was when I had a truly unattractive finished piece (which is much harder to accomplish than you would think). This piece had too many colors and fibers going every which way. I couldn't think of anything to do with it. So I cut the piece into simple squares. As I examined the squares individually, each one was a work of art! I actually fell in love with all the pieces. This unattractive piece of silk fusion was the catalyst that began my exploration into mosaics. I sorted the pieces by color and intensity, and rearranged them on a black background using bold red pieces as the focus of

SILK FUSION

my design, gently curving across the background fabric. I realized that the original piece of silk fusion was actually quite valuable.

After that experience, I became bolder and began cutting up even my most beautiful pieces to use in more intricate mosaics. I like to use about three different-colored pieces of silk fusion in my mosaics to create a balanced and exciting design.

Extra pieces and scraps are perfect for gift cards and gift tags, so don't throw anything away!

MOSAIC BASICS

For a successful mosaic, use a variety of shapes and sizes. Use squares set on point, rectangles used vertically or horizontally. Lay out straight-sided shapes in a curved pattern. Negative space is a very important element of the mosaic design, so be sure to leave some larger parts of your design free of silk fusion. You can also create negative space by placing some shapes further apart.

I have never used circular pieces in my mosaics because they are hard to cut out. I imagine you could use a die-cut machine to accomplish this if you want to use many circles in your mosaic.

Always begin your project by first applying fusible web to the back of the silk fusion pieces you will be using.

You can use whatever shapes inspire you to create your mosaic. To demonstrate some basic construction ideas, follow along as I put together a piece based on one of my favorite subjects: poppies.

I start by making a pattern of a poppy flower head on tracing paper. I place the pattern over the piece of silk fusion I wish to use. Notice how the details of the silk fusion show through the tracing paper, allowing me to place it over elements I want to include in the poppy. Before cutting the shape out, I affix fusible web to the back of the silk fusion piece. I do not need to cut the pattern from the paper first, just cut both pieces at the same time. Next, I cut the piece into smaller shapes. If I spread all the pieces out now, the final

ABOVE: *Small pieces of silk fusion are perfect for composing mosaics. I used these squares in two pieces of art work shown in the Gallery: "Silk Squared" (page 76) and "Gold Silk Squared" (page 84).*

Step by Step

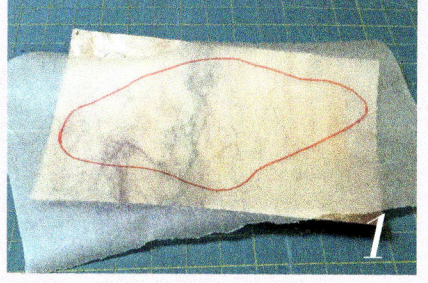 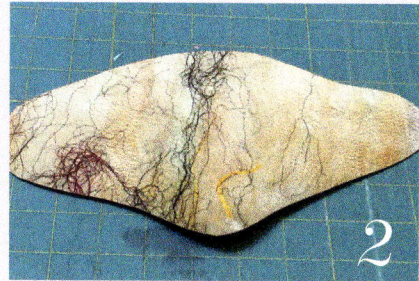 

1. I start by making a pattern of a poppy flower head on tracing paper. 2. Using the tracing paper pattern, I cut the shape from silk fusion. 3. I cut the shape into smaller pieces, then trim a small amount off each small piece to create areas where the background fabric shows through.

 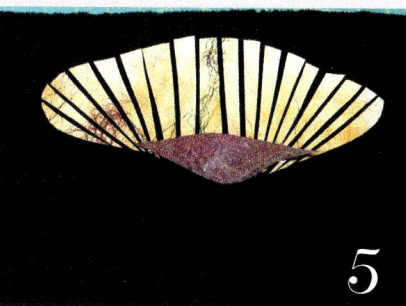 

4. To add another element to the base of the flower, I draw the base onto the original flower head pattern. Placing the pattern over a new piece of silk fusion, I cut the piece out. 5. The piece will sit at the base of the flower. 6. The base is cut into smaller pieces.

7. Smaller pieces are trimmed and some of the pieces are shortened from their original length so that all the pieces flow together. At this point, since I am satisfied with this flower head, I iron it into place. 8. Now it's time to add additional flower heads. 9. Using another tracing paper pattern, I cut a silk fusion piece for the second flower.

10. The flower head and base are cut into smaller pieces and trimmed following the same steps as the first flower. I have included negative space in the patterns to represent the flower stems. 11. Another paper pattern shows the shape of the third flower head. 12. With the three major portions of the composition complete and ironed in place, it's time to move on to the mosaic's background pieces.

Step by Step

13. I cut 1-inch strips from one piece of silk fusion (selecting an interesting area that moves through at least two colors). This will be a long line of mosaic pieces, so I cut three strips. 14. Each strip is cut into pieces measuring about 1 inch square. I leave the pieces on the cutting board as cut and in order, so they are ready to be transferred to the background fabric in that same order and orientation.

configuration would be larger than the pattern piece, so I cut a small amount off of each sub-piece, creating areas where the background fabric shows through. At this point, I have not ironed anything down, because I want to make sure my next element fits onto this one.

To add another element to the flower, I begin with the original pattern with the new element drawn onto it. I place the pattern over a new piece of silk fusion (with fusible web already applied to the back) and cut the piece out. I further cut the piece apart, leaving space for the background fabric and then shorten some of the pieces from the original shape so that all the pieces flow together. At this point, since I am satisfied with this flower head, I iron it into place.

I then add a second and third flower head with patterns for each. I have included negative space in the patterns to represent the flower stems.

One of the design elements I use in my mosaics is to keep cut pieces in their original orientation and relationship. For example, when making the curved line of squares shown in photo 14 at left, I cut a 1-inch strip from one piece of silk fusion (selecting an area that moves through at least two colors). I then cut this 1-inch strip down into 1-inch square pieces. I leave the pieces on the cutting board as cut and in order. I then transfer each piece to my background fabric in that same order and orientation, leaving generally equal-sized space between them. When I'm creating a curve, these spaces will vary. This orientation gives the line continuity. If I mixed these pieces up and then placed them, the line would feel much different.

I don't get too caught up in cutting each piece for the mosaic absolutely perfectly. The example I mentioned above involves using a line created with 1-by-1-inch pieces. I will use a straight-edge to cut a perfect 1-inch strip, but when cutting the individual 1-inch squares, I just use my eye and cut without a straight edge. The individual squares might not be perfect, but differences are not noticeable in the final product, and it is much less labor-intensive and faster to eyeball the smaller cuts.

I use tweezers to transfer the small pieces from the cutting board to the background piece.

15. Some squares need to be further trimmed to fit in tight spaces, such as where the flower pieces come together. You can mark the cuts you need to make, or just estimate and cut. 16. The first row of background squares is complete and wraps around the flower heads. The darker background squares make the flowers pop.

SILK FUSION

Step by Step

17. Squares for the second row of background were made by cutting ½-inch strips and then cutting those strips into ½-inch squares. 18. I made the third row of pieces by cutting 1-inch strips and then cutting those strips into ¼-inch rectangles. Using different colors for each row keeps the artwork lively.

The idea may seem daunting and tedious, but you will gain dexterity quickly using this method.

As I work my way around the edges of the flowers to create the background, some squares need to be further trimmed to fit into the design, such as in the tight corners where flower pieces come together. I do this by eye, or by marking the piece that needs to be trimmed with a Frixion Pen (made by Pilot and found at office supply stores). The ink of Frixion Pens disappears when heat is applied, so when the piece is ironed in place, any remaining marks will disappear. Sometimes I will just use a permanent marker, then take care to cut the entire mark off the piece.

I fill in more background by adding more lines (or layers), each layer using a new color of silk fusion, and a different shape for individual pieces. I make the second layer by cutting ½-inch strips and then cutting those strips into ½-inch squares. To make the third layer, I cut 1-inch strips and then cut those strips into ¼-inch rectangles.

SILK FUSION

To fill in a small open area, I lay a piece of tracing paper over the space to fill. (The open space can be seen through the paper.) I draw a line around this open space onto the paper, leaving a small space for background fabric to show through. Now I place the traced shape over the piece of silk fusion I will be using and cut the shape out.

I can use the cut shape as is, or further cut the piece into smaller shapes. I leave pieces, as cut, on the cutting board so I can figure out how they go back together. When cutting the shape down further, a small amount must then be cut off each smaller piece to make space for the background fabric to show through.

Once the mosaic pieces are all ironed in place, the piece is ready for stitching.

STITCHING AND QUILTING

Next, the pieces must be topstitched down with a sewing machine. Using black thread allows the stitching to almost disappear into the black background fabric. The goal is to catch every piece of the mosaic with stitch. Sometimes you can accomplish this with a straight

19. To plan for pieces to fill a small open area, I put a piece of tracing paper over the space. (The open space can be seen through the paper.) 20. I trace the open space onto the paper, leaving area around it for background fabric to show through. 21. Now I place the traced shape over a piece of silk fusion and cut the shape out. 22. I can use the entire cut shape or cut it into smaller shapes, as shown in 23.

SILK FUSION

24. With all the mosaic pieces ironed in place, I added stitching. Some of the pieces are held down at both the top and bottom with one continuous line of stitching, while others have one line of stitching running through the middle. There are no set rules, but I try to catch every piece with stitch.

line of stitching, such as when squares are aligned. If you have a very small piece to sew down, or if you are sewing down an area that has been created using the true mosaic method, simply make sure that at least a corner has been caught with stitching.

Notice that some of the pieces are held down at both the top and bottom of the pieces with one continuous line of stitching, while others have one line of stitching going right through the middle. The mosaic pieces are held down with several continuous lines of stitching. There is no correct way to do this: think of it as another design element.

After topstitching is complete, you may consider quilting the piece. To do this, create a sandwich with batting and a piece of fabric for the backing, sized as large as your finished mosaic. Using black thread, simply stitch between design elements onto background fabric; not on top of silk fusion pieces. This will allow the design elements to come forward, just like with traditional quilting.

USING ANGELINA

You can also use pieces of prepared Angelina web in your

Tip

Sometimes when ironing a piece of thick silk fusion to the background fabric, the heat does not penetrate all the way through to properly set the glue of the fusible. To ensure good adherence, once your design is complete and secured in place, turn the piece over and iron from the back.

mosaic pieces to add that wonderful sparkle and shine. I find I use it in almost every piece I create. To use, apply fusible web to a large piece of prepared Angelina, then cut pieces out and use in the same way as the silk fusion.

Angelina is very heat-sensitive. If too much heat is applied, it will lose its sparkle. Because of this, it is a good idea to add Angelina pieces toward the end of the project if possible. Always use an applique pressing sheet or parchment paper on Angelina because it and the fusible medium underneath will stick to the iron.

FUSIBLE WEB TIPS

There are many types of fusible web available. On page 14, I explain the differences and my experience with fusible web.

Inevitably, fusible medium will stick to your applique pressing sheet and/or parchment paper. This usually happens when you pull the pressing sheet off the ironed fusible web before it is completely cool. Check your sheet each time you use it by rubbing your hand over the side coming in contact with the fusible medium. You can rub off any bits left with your hand or by scrubbing with a wet or dry sponge. If you don't remove fusible residue from the sheet, the next time you use it, the fusible medium will either transfer to the top of your project or to your iron.

Be careful to get all fusing scraps off the ironing surface and into the trash.

If you do get fusible medium on your iron, you can use an iron cleaner such as Bo Nash Iron Clean, Mr. Clean Magic Eraser or Iron Clean Sheets. Iron Clean Sheets are the same as dryer sheets used in the laundry, such as Cling-Free, so I prefer to use dryer sheets. Just glide the iron over the dryer sheet to release the fusible medium and then on a scrap of fabric to remove any oily residue. Using a dryer sheet has the added benefit of leaving a nice clean smell in the studio, but some people find the aroma too strong. Be sure to use a non-scented dryer sheet if you are sensitive to the fragrance. Sometimes a bit of scrubbing with a non-scratch scrubbing sponge is necessary to clean an iron.

TRUE MOSAIC PIECING

One method to fill in larger areas is true mosaic piecing like you see in mosaic tiling. This method takes much more time and patience, but the effect is wonderful. True mosaic piecing is accomplished when all the spaces between cut pieces are of uniform size. To create this look, freely cut some silk fusion (I usually use just one cohesive piece of silk fusion) into many sizes and shapes. Then begin placing pieces like a puzzle, finding pieces that fit perfectly into open spaces. If you find one that almost fits, but not quite, you can trim it to fit. Make your cuts by eye or place the almost-perfect piece in its space, and draw a line on the silk fusion piece where you need to cut. A permanent marker works well to mark the cutting lines. Cut to the inside of the line so that the marker does not show. Again, you can also use a Frixion Pen to mark the line and it will disappear when you iron the piece in place. As the space fills in, more precision cutting will need to take place.

To create the mosaic pieced art shown on page 47, I cut one piece of silk fusion that was somewhat homogenous in color into many different shapes. I began by using the flat side of pieces to create a crisp line on the outside of the design element. Once I was happy with the outside shape, I ironed them in place and carefully began to fit other pieces to fill in the shape, ironing them in place as often as possible.

Once the mosaic design piece was completed, I began work on the background. By using a different set of colors for the background and also a different mosaic process, the original design element really stands out. The mosaic piecing took twice as long to create as it took to add the background elements to complete the piece! I would like to point out that when I created this piece I did not first create a pattern. I had an idea of the general shape I was after, so I just began creating an outline and adjusted the shape with my tweezers until the shape was to my liking.

Sometimes I use a pattern and sometimes I don't: there are certainly no rules that apply here. Since this was the first design element placed, I didn't have any constraints, so I just let go and gave my creativity full rein.

Once true mosaic pieces are fused to the background I stitch them in place as described on page 43.

ABOVE: *This piece, "Shamen," was created using hundreds of pieces of silk fusion and Angelina that were fused and stitched to a cotton background.*

True Mosaic Piecing Step by Step

1. To begin this traditionally pieced mosaic, I started with a circle shape made with Angelina. 2. I used the flat side of the mosaic pieces to create the crisp line on the outside of the design element. Once I was happy with the outside shape, I ironed the pieces in place and carefully began to fit other pieces to fill in the shape, ironing them in place as often as possible. This piece was created without a pattern. I had an idea of the general shape I was after, so I created an outline and adjusted the shape with tweezers. 3. Next, I tackled the background. By using a different set of pieces and also a different mosaic process, the original design element stands out. 4. By using black thread, the stitching almost disappears into the black background fabric. The goal is to catch every piece of the mosaic with stitch.

Cards and Tags

SUPPLIES
Bone folder
Sewing machine
Iron

MATERIALS
Silk fusion scraps

Card stock

Ribbon

Making cards is fast and fun, and a great way to use all of your silk fusion scraps. Just make sure that any scrap you use has fusible web already applied to the back. Silk fusion pieces may then be "glued" to card stock directly with your iron. Your card can be further embellished with machine or hand stitching, but that is not necessary to hold the silk fusion to the paper.

When working with a larger piece of silk fusion, such as in the Christmas tree card (opposite), using a piece of batting between the silk fusion and the card stock adds a textural quilted effect to the card. The silk fusion was sewn to the card stock in this example. Always add all embellishments before folding cards in half. Tags benefit from a bit of ribbon attached to a corner.

SILK FUSION

Gift Envelope

SUPPLIES
Cutting mat, rotary cutter and straight edge
Scissors
Sewing machine
Basic sewing supplies

MATERIALS
Cotton fabric for lining in size necessary for your envelope dimensions

Silk fusion in size necessary for your envelope dimensions

Matching thread

Snap (optional)

This pattern comes together so fast; I like to whip out a few at a time, giving me instant gratification and a sense of accomplishment. This is also a great general envelope pattern and can be enlarged to any size to fit a greeting card, check or other items.

The pattern on page 52 creates an envelope that is the perfect size for credit cards.

SILK FUSION

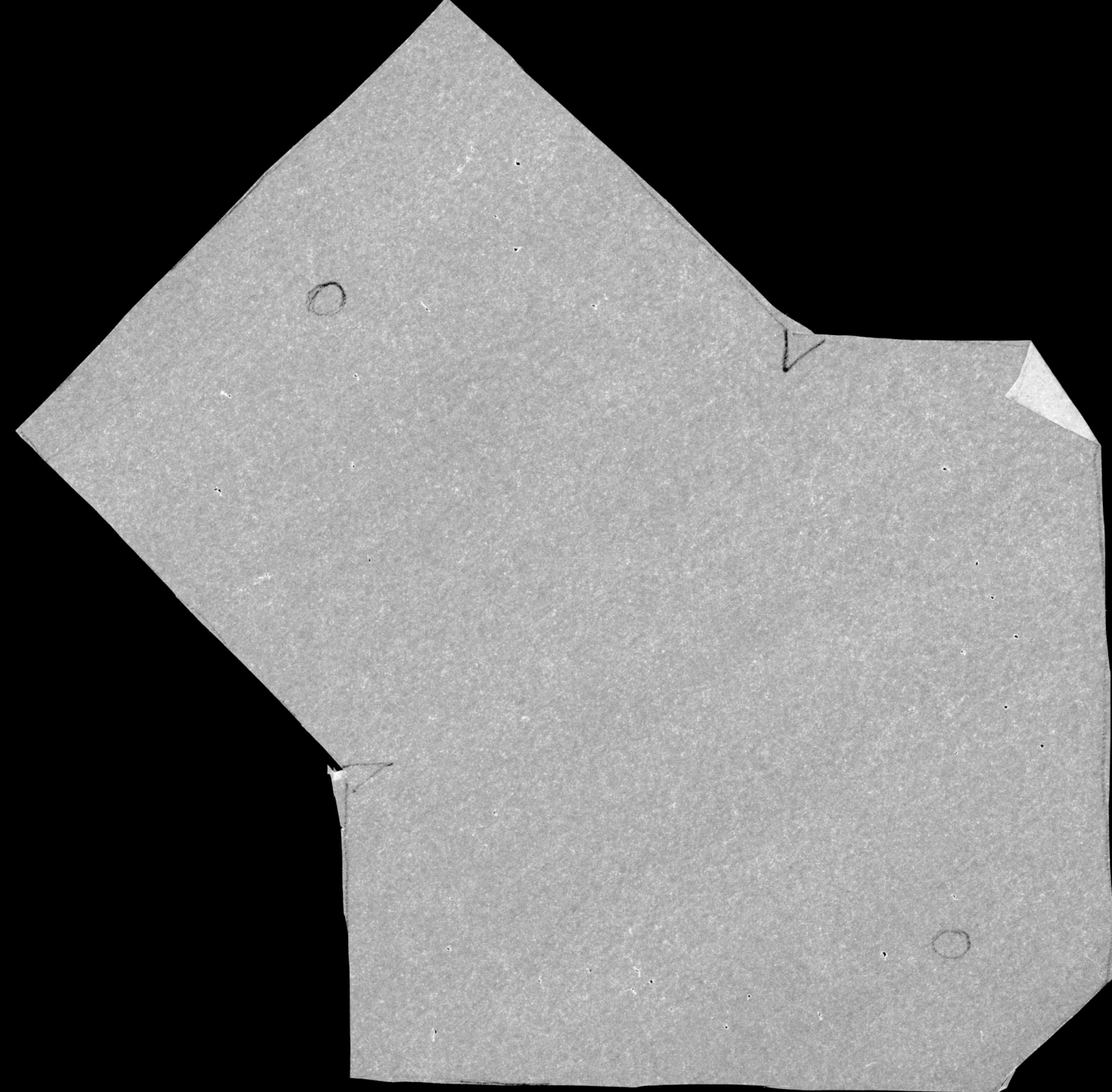

1. Make a copy of the pattern on paper and cut it out. Using the pattern as a guide, cut out a piece of silk fusion and a piece of coordinating or contrasting fabric for the lining.

2. If you want to use a snap, attach it first, using the pattern as a guide for placement. Snaps are attached to the right side of the silk fusion. I usually apply a small reinforcement piece of fabric to the back of the silk fusion and attach the snap to both pieces to strengthen against the pulling required to open the snap. Attaching the snap is really the most arduous part of the construction of this envelope, and not particularly necessary, so I usually don't bother. Tucking the envelope away in your purse, backpack or back pocket is all that is necessary for the flap to stay closed and in place.

3. Place silk fusion and lining fabric right sides together and sew around edges indicated on the pattern, leaving the two longest edges open. Use a ¼-inch seam.

4. Turn right side out through one of the openings and press seams. You can topstitch a scant ⅛ inch around each of the pressed edges, but it is not necessary.

5. Fold one of the unsewn edges in half, with the right sides of silk fusion together and stitch using a ¼-inch seam. Repeat for the other unsewn edge

6. Clip corners, turn seams right side out, and press new seams to the middle to create the finished envelope.

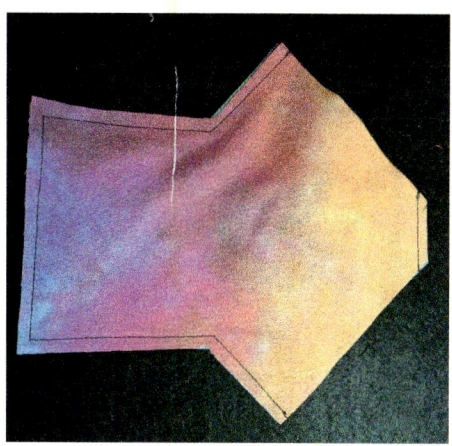

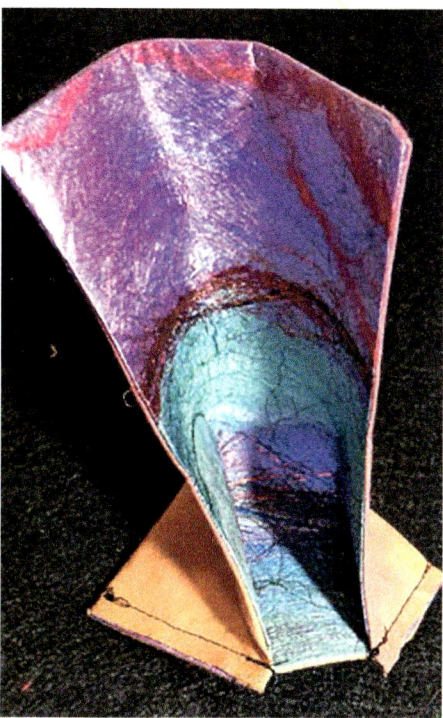

TOP: *One envelope piece is cut from both silk fusion and lining fabric.* MIDDLE: *Seams are sewn on the top, sides and bottom, according to the pattern, with the diagonal sides left open.* ABOVE: *After turning the piece right side out, the envelope is folded to sew the diagonal seams.*

SILK FUSION

Gift Envelope Pattern

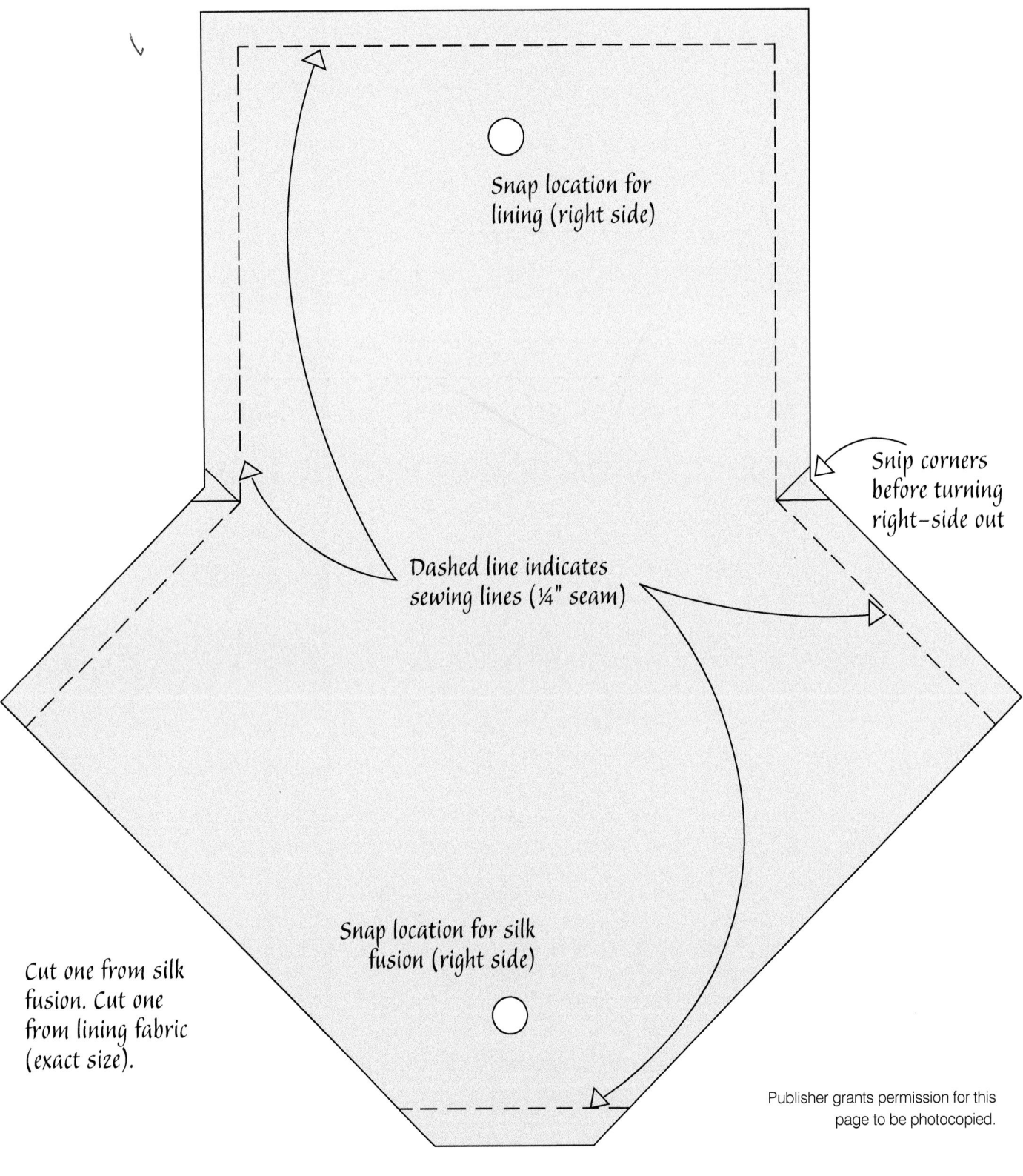

Decorative Boxes

SUPPLIES
Rotary cutter, mat and straight edge
Scissors
Sewing machine
Basic sewing supplies

MATERIALS
Two pieces of silk fusion (for the small 1½-by-2-inch box shown here, silk fusion pieces should be at least 6 by 6 inches)

Two pieces of felt 6 by 6 inches

Matching thread

Your choice of beads, buttons, embroidery floss or other embellishment to use as a handle for the box top

These adorable boxes are easy to make. The top of the box is a bit larger than the bottom so the two pieces fit snugly together.

SILK FUSION

...... Notes ......

Use the pattern provided on page 55 or your own pattern based on the box's basic dimensions. By creating your own pattern, you can make the box as tall or shallow as you wish. The top of your box should be at least ½ inch larger than the bottom, (see notes on the pattern page for more information.)

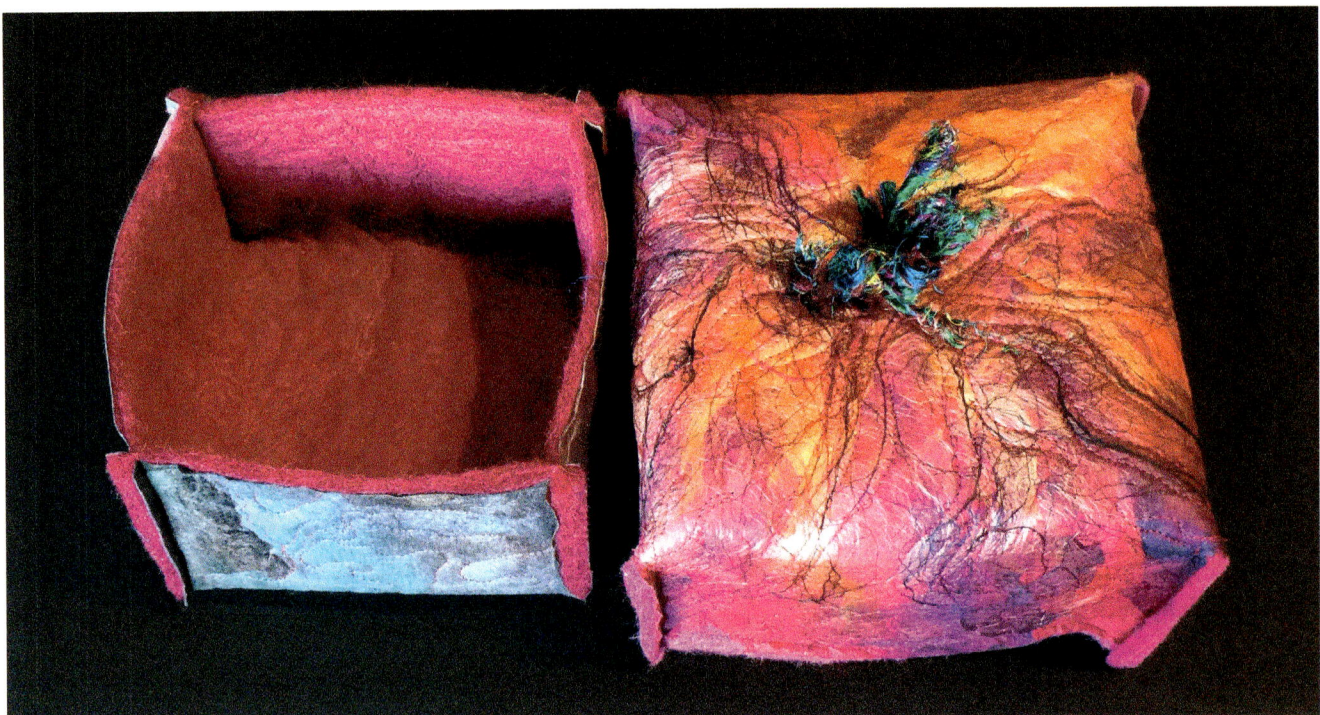

For this box, you will need one piece of silk fusion and one piece of colorful felt cut to equal size, for both the top and bottom boxes. I prefer to cut the pieces out of the silk fusion and the felt at the same time to create a crisply aligned edge.

1. Pin one piece of silk fusion to one piece of felt with wrong sides together. Cut around the pattern piece. Repeat with the other pattern piece.

2. Stitch around all edges of both the box top and box bottom ¼ inch in from the edges to hold the layers together. Now you can remove the pins and add embellishments, if you wish, like machine stitching, embroidery or beading.

3. To make a pull or handle on the top of the box, create a simple loop, or add a bead, button or other embellishment that is easy to grasp at the center of the box top (as marked).

4. Sew each of the four corner edges together to form the box shape. Do this for both the box top and bottom. Use a ¼-inch seam with wrong sides together, leaving the seam allowances on the outside as a decorative element.

5. Slide the completed box top over the bottom.

SILK FUSION

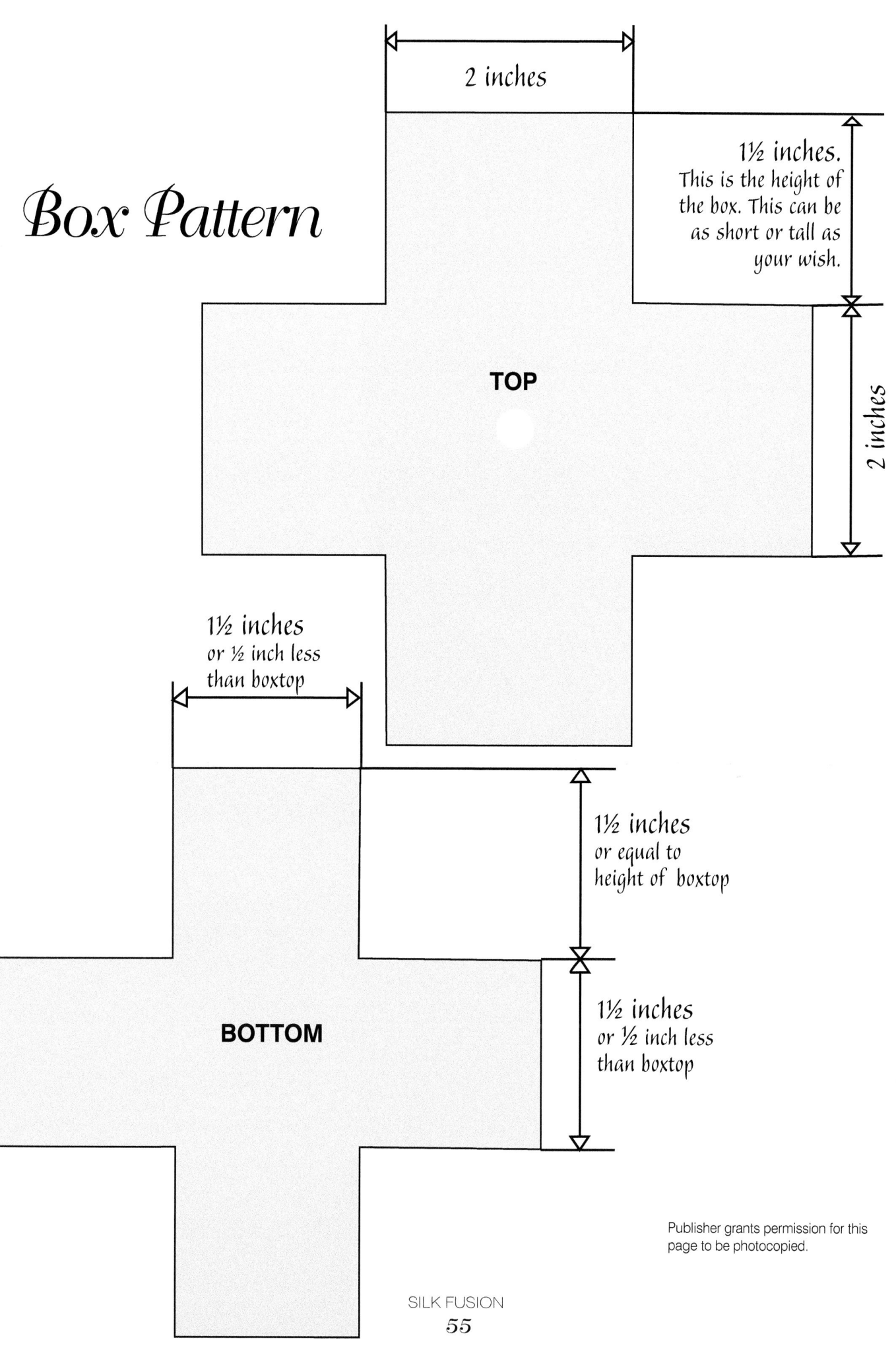

Sketchbook or Journal

SUPPLIES
Rotary cutter and mat
Scissors
Bone folder (optional)
Large embroidery needle or awl
Ruler

MATERIALS
Silk fusion

Batting (optional)

Paper or cardstock

Button or embellishment

Matching thread

Yarn, floss or pearl cotton to bind pages

String or ribbon to tie journal closed

There are so many ways to make a sketchbook or journal. You can easily cover a purchased sketchbook with silk fusion, but this is another way to construct a journal from scratch, pages and all, for a truly original and heartfelt creation.

These journals are fun to embellish and if you are feeling a little creative, you can color the paper pages before inserting them. I learned the technique of bookmaking with pre-decorated pages from my favorite mixed media artist, Judith Cassel-Mamet. You can see examples of her amazing work at www.jcmamet.net.

1. First decide on how large the insert pages will be. The size may be dictated by the paper you have on hand. Note that the paper you use will be folded in half for construction purposes, so if you start with 8½-by-11-inch paper, after folding, it will measure 8½ by 5 ½ inches. If you start with 9 x12 inch paper, after folding, it will be 9 by 6 inches, and a 5-by-7-inch piece will end up measuring 5 by 3½ inches.

2. A bone folder is quite helpful when folding sheets of paper in half. To use, place a ruler on the paper where you want the fold. Hold the ruler firmly in place with one hand. Run the pointed tip of the bone folder along the length of the ruler, pressing it firmly down as you go. Fold the scored paper along the crease you've made. Press the fold flat with the heel of your hand. Run the edge of the broad side of the bone folder along the fold and press gently. The end result should be a sharp and neat fold in the paper or cardstock.

3. Depending on the thickness of the paper, divide folded pages into groups of four, (making eight pages) and keep the pages folded as a group. (For thick paper, it may be better to put pages in groups of three.) Four groups of folded paper yields 32 finished pages, and requires about one inch of width at the spine of the cover. Each group of folded pages will be hand-sewn to the silk fusion spine of the cover.

4. Next, consider cover construction options. If you use just one layer of silk fusion, both the front and back of the piece will show. If two layers of silk fusion are used, only the front of each piece will show, but the cover will be stronger and more substantial. You can also construct a quilted "sandwich" of three layers. My favorite construction, because of the way it feels in my hands when holding the book, is two pieces of silk fusion sewn together. If you have a particularly thick piece of fusion, or a piece of silk fusion made using the varnish textile medium, one layer may be sufficient.

5. Calculate the dimensions of the finished cover. It should be ½ inch larger in length and width than the paper you use, before folding, with an additional 1 inch lengthwise for the book spine. The additional ½ inch will leave you with ¼ inch overlap on all sides. (Remember, the size of the book spine is determined by

ABOVE: *Four signatures of folded paper are ready to be bound into a silk fusion sketchbook cover.*

the number of folded pages included. More pages will require a thicker spine.) For example, if you start with 8½-by-11-inch paper, after folding, it will measure **8½ by 5½** inches, so the size of the cover piece would be 12½ (**5 ½ + 5½** + ½ + 1) inches by 9 (**8½ + ½**). If you start with 9-by-12-inch paper, after folding, it will be **9 by 6** inches, so the size of the cover piece would be 13½ (**6 + 6** + ½ + 1) inches by 9½ (**9** + ½) inches. A 5-by-7-inch piece of paper folded in half is **5 by 3½** inches and the size of the cover piece would be 8½ (**3 ½ + 3 ½** + ½ + 1) inches by 5½ (**5** + ½).

6. If using two layers of silk fusion or the quilted three-layer cover, you will need to sew the layers together, so add another ½ inch to the length and width of your final cover dimensions to account for seam allowances. For example, if you start with 8½-by-11-inch paper, after folding, it will measure **8½ by 5½** inches, so the size of the cover piece would be 13 (**5½ + 5½** + ½ + 1+½) inches by 9½ (**8½** + ½+½). If you start with 9-by-12-inch paper, after folding, it will be **9 by 6** inches, so the size of the cover piece would be 14 (**6 + 6** + ½ + 1+ ½) inches by 10 (**9** + ½+ ½) inches. A 5-by-7-inch piece of paper folded in half is **5 by 3½** inches, so the size of the cover piece would be 9 (**3½ + 3½** + ½ + 1 + ½) inches by 6 (**5** + ½ + ½).

7. If using two layers, sew the pieces of silk fusion with right sides together using a ¼-inch seam. Stitch around all four sides, leaving a 3-inch opening on one edge for turning. Trim corners, turn right side out and press. Top stitch all the way around the cover a scant ⅛ inch from the edge, being careful to fold the seam allowances at the turning hole to the inside and closing them with stitching. Quilt or embellish as desired.

8. To construct a quilted three-layer cover, cut two pieces of silk fusion and one piece of batting to the calculated size (or use one piece of silk fusion, one piece of batting and one piece of fabric for the backing). Layer silk fusion right sides together and place the batting on top of the backside of one of your silk fusion pieces. Sew around all four sides through all three layers using a ¼-inch seam. Leave a 3-inch opening on one edge for turning. Trim corners, turn right side out and press. Top stitch all the way around a scant 1/8 inch from the edge, being careful to fold the seam allowances at the turning hole to the inside and closing them with stitching. Quilt or embellish as desired.

9. You are now ready to hand stitch your pages to your cover.

To delineate your book spine area, press two folds in the cover with your iron, one inch apart, and equidistant from the center line of your cover. This one-inch space is the spine. If you like, you can use a pencil or pen to mark these lines on the inside of the cover. Your folded papers will be sewn into this spine so the marking lines will not show. If you have four folded groups of paper, this one inch of spine must be further subdivided into five spaces or four lines. (See illustration opposite.)

10. Line up all the folded, four-page sets of paper and mark each one for stitching location as shown in the illustration opposite. There will be four marks, equal distance apart, and 1 inch from the top and bottom edge of the paper. The four holes will yield two tie points for each folded set on the spine. For books smaller than 4 inches, two marks 1 inch apart

Hole Placement

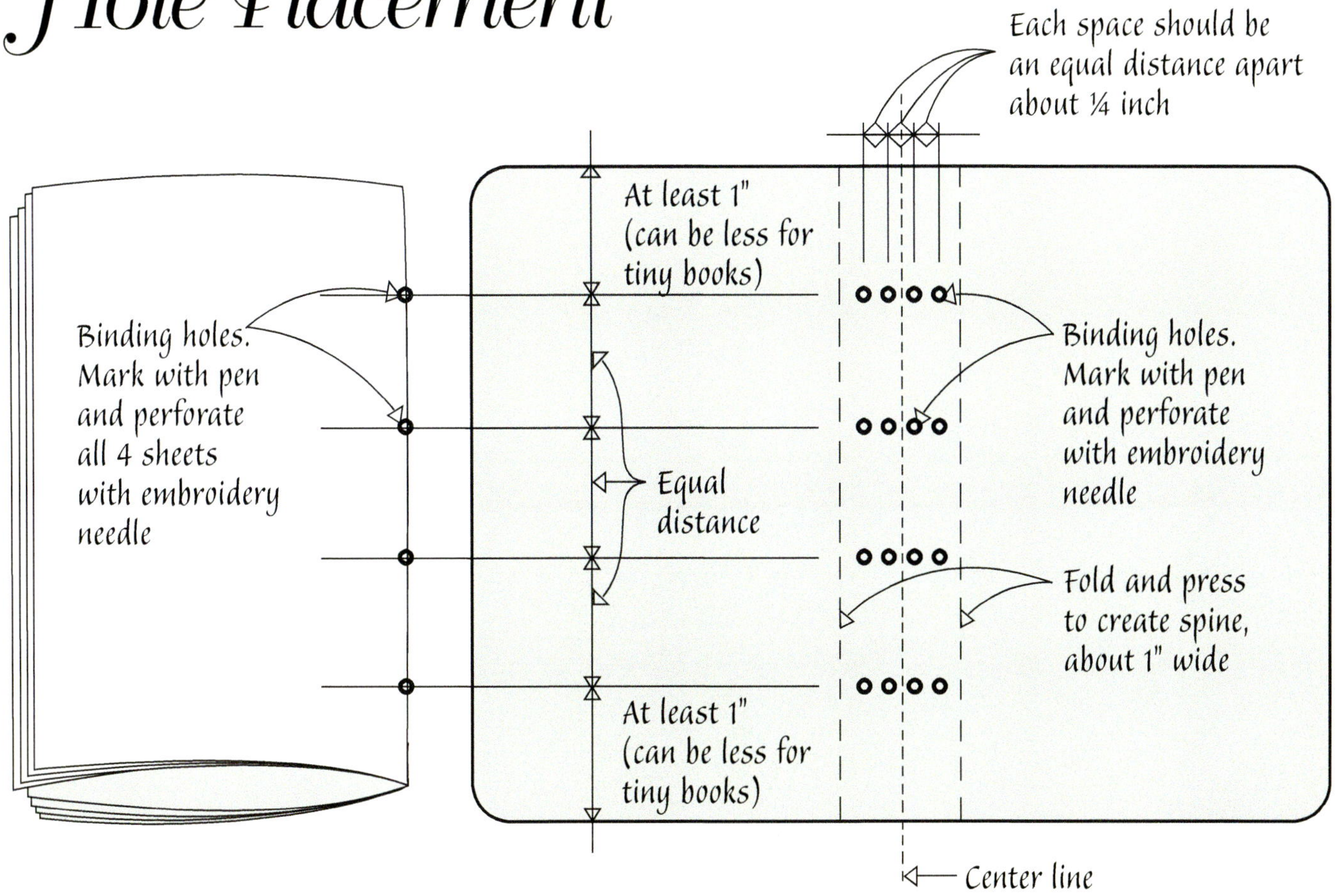

Each space should be an equal distance apart about ¼ inch

At least 1" (can be less for tiny books)

Binding holes. Mark with pen and perforate all 4 sheets with embroidery needle

Equal distance

Binding holes. Mark with pen and perforate with embroidery needle

Fold and press to create spine, about 1" wide

At least 1" (can be less for tiny books)

Center line

ABOVE: *Folded paper inserts are bound into the silk fusion cover.*

SILK FUSION

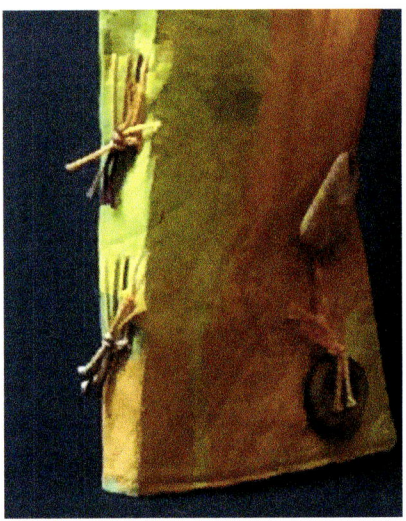

ABOVE LEFT: *Binding ties are knottted on the outside spine of this small book.* ABOVE RIGHT: *A simple ring binding holds this silk fusion journal together.*

are sufficient. Now place one of the folded paper sets inside the cover and centered from top to bottom. Using the marks you made on the paper, transfer the location of the holes to the cover. Make a dot on the spine at the intersection of the hole in the paper and the lines on the spine.

I like to pre "drill" my paper with a large needle to make stitching easier. Simply push a large needle, such as an embroidery needle, through all four pieces of paper at the dots you made. There should be four holes.

11. You can bind the book with any kind of thread or yarn you desire. My favorite is pearl cotton. It is easily accessible, comes in a range of colors and is easy to use with an embroidery needle. Make sure to use a needle that is large enough for the thread or yarn you choose.

With your threaded needle, begin attaching grouped pages to the spine. Start with about 8 inches of thread. (You do not need to knot this thread.) Beginning at the bottom set of holes, bring your needle from the outside of the book spine through to the inside of the spine and then through the bottom hole in the back side of the grouped pages. Go back through the next hole 1 inch away on the grouped pages, and then back through the book spine from the inside to the outside. Tie the two ends together on the outside of the book spine. With another 8 inches of thread, pull the thread through the top set of two holes in the grouped folded pages in the same manner and tie. Repeat for each group of folded pages.

12. For smaller books, consider binding in the following manner: Instead of four vertical holes in the spine and folded pages, use three evenly spaced holes. When hand stitching the cover to pages, bring your needle from the outside of the book spine through the middle hole, then through the middle hole of the folded pages. Go back through the bottom holes of folded page sets and spine to the outside of the book spine, then past the middle hole to the top hole of the spine, through book spine and pages, and finally back through the middle holes in the folded pages again to the outside of the spine.

Both thread ends will now be coming out of the middle hole at the outside cover. Tie together.

13. Add a tie closure for your book if you wish by sewing on a button or bead and some ribbon, twine or leather lacing.

Purses

Take your silk fusion with you! This basic purse pattern can be used with any textile. The pattern instructions include an easy zipper installation, and the design works in any size or shape. There are no set dimensions for this pattern: Start with whatever size of silk fusion piece you have. Choose the simple pattern with no lining or, for a more polished look, follow the pattern that includes a lining.

Unlined Purse

SUPPLIES
Rotary cutter and mat or scissors
Ruler
Sewing machine
Basic sewing supplies

MATERIALS
Silk fusion in size necessary for your purse dimensions.

Zipper in length necessary for your purse dimensions

Matching thread

Your choice of beads, buttons, embroidery floss or other embellishment

Purse strap made of chain, fabric or crocheted yarn, in your desired length

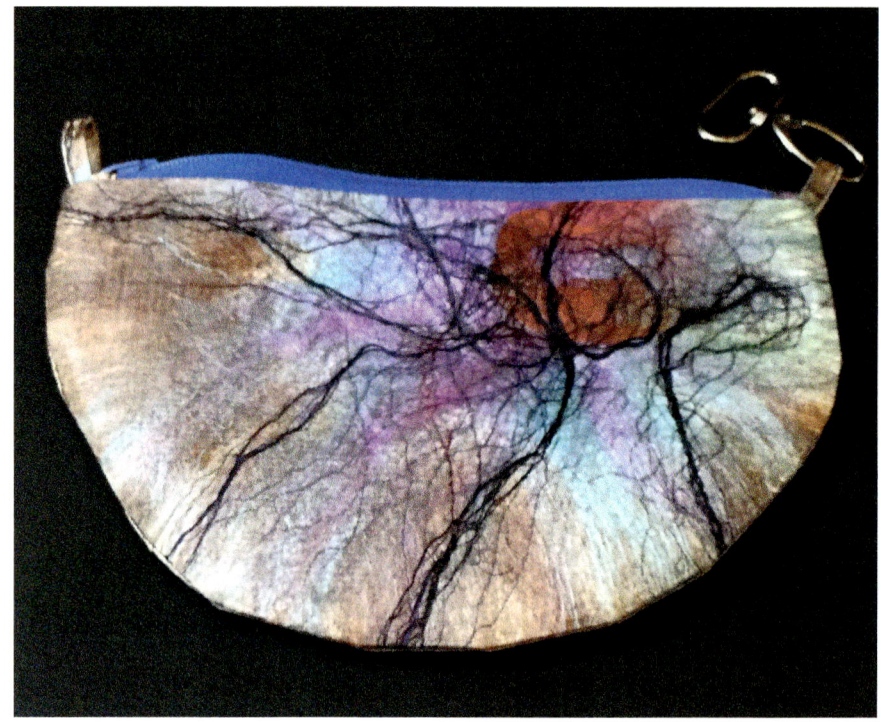

The best thing about using silk fusion with this pattern is that silk fusion does not fray at cut edges, and because there is no lining, you can open the purse to see the other side of your silk fusion piece.

1. Draw a pattern or decide on dimensions for your purse front and back. You can use two rectangular pieces, two squares or you can add a curve to the sides or the bottom. Your purse can be any size or shape, but the front and back pieces should be equal in size and shape.

2. Add any embellishments to the piece of silk fusion, such as stitching or beading, before construction of the purse begins.

3. Before cutting the purse

front and back pattern pieces from your piece of silk fusion, cut a ½-by-6-inch strip out of the piece for zipper binding and optional purse loops.

4. To create a binding piece for both ends of the zipper, fold the ½-by-6-inch strip of silk fusion in half, lengthwise. Press. Cut two, 1-inch pieces from the binding strip.

5. To give the completed purse a neat finished look, I prepare the zipper following this process I adapted from Atkinson Designs. First trim the top edges of the zipper tape, leaving ¼ inch of the zipper ends from the first teeth.

Then cut the zipper on the opposite end 1 inch shorter than the length of the top of the purse. When adding purse loops, the zipper should be cut 1½ inches shorter than the length of the top of the purse. If necessary, cut the end of the zipper right through the teeth (with utility scissors).

6. Unzip the zipper a few inches and machine stitch across the tape to hold the two halves together near the top zipper stops.

Now, slide this end of the zipper into the fold of the 1-inch piece of binding strip and sew the open edges of the binding strip together, catching the

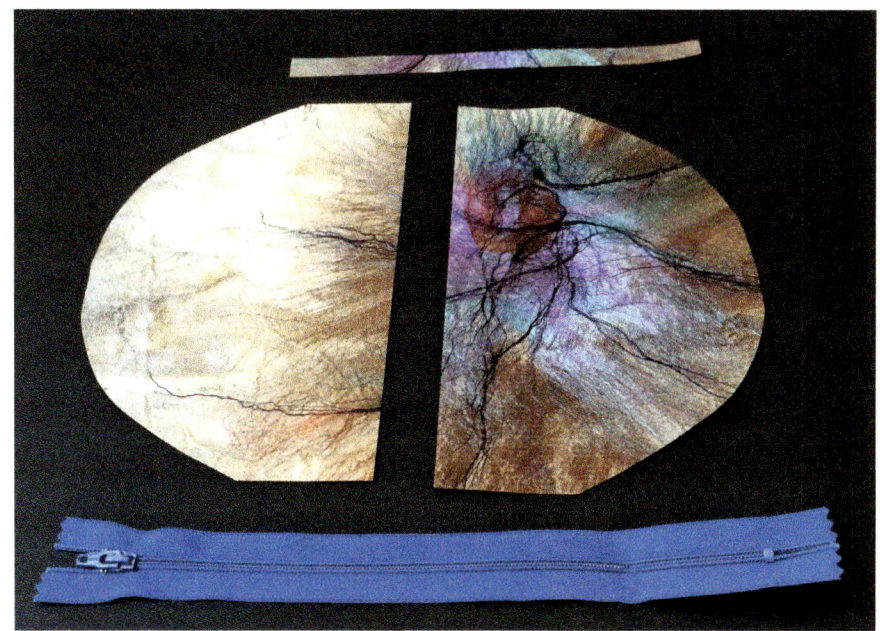

ABOVE: *Matching front and back pieces of the unlined purse are ready for the zipper installation. A narrow strip of silk fusion will be used for the zipper binding and purse loops.*

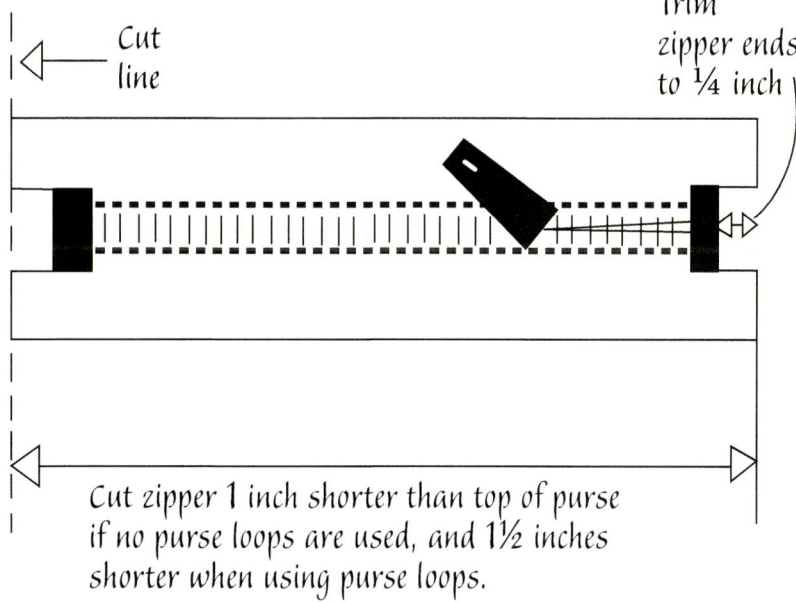

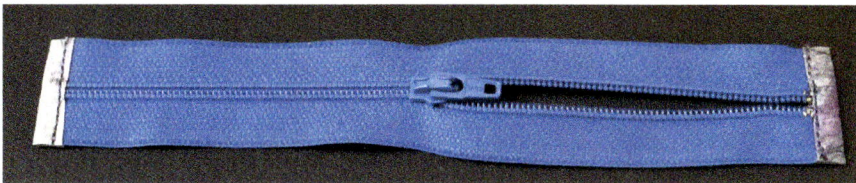

ABOVE: *After the zipper is trimmed a folded piece of silk fusion is sewn to each end of the zipper.*

SILK FUSION

zipper between.

Attach the other 1-inch binding piece to the other end of the zipper in the same fashion. (Your sewing machine will sew right through the teeth; but sew slowly.)

7. Purse loops are handy because they allow for any type of handle attachment. Snap hooks attach easily, or a folded fabric or crocheted strap can be easily attached. If you want purse loops, cut the remaining folded strip into two, 2-inch pieces. Topstitch along the edge of each folded piece as close to the edge as possible.

8. To install zipper into purse, place zipper in the center of the top of one purse piece, right sides together (with zipper pull facing down), with the ends of the zipper, ½ inch in from the side edge of the purse. If you include purse loops, align raw edges of the loops with raw edge of purse top ½ inch in from the side edge of the purse and alongside the ends of the zipper. The length of loop should hang down toward the inside of purse.

Sew loops and zipper onto the top edge of the purse piece with a ¼-inch seam.

With most zippers, it is hard to

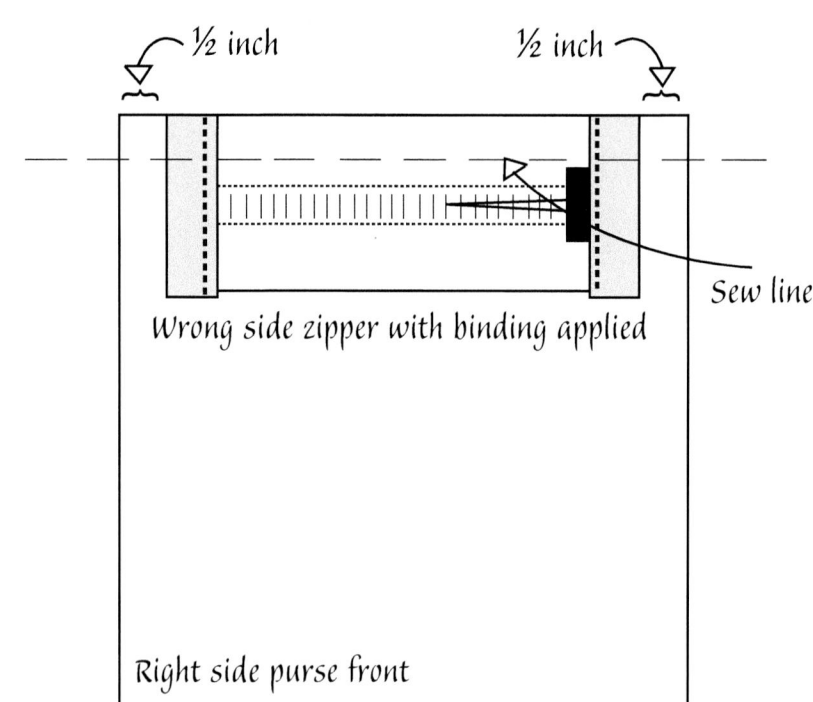

ABOVE: *Zipper in place face down at top of purse front and ready to be attached. This purse does not include purse loops.*

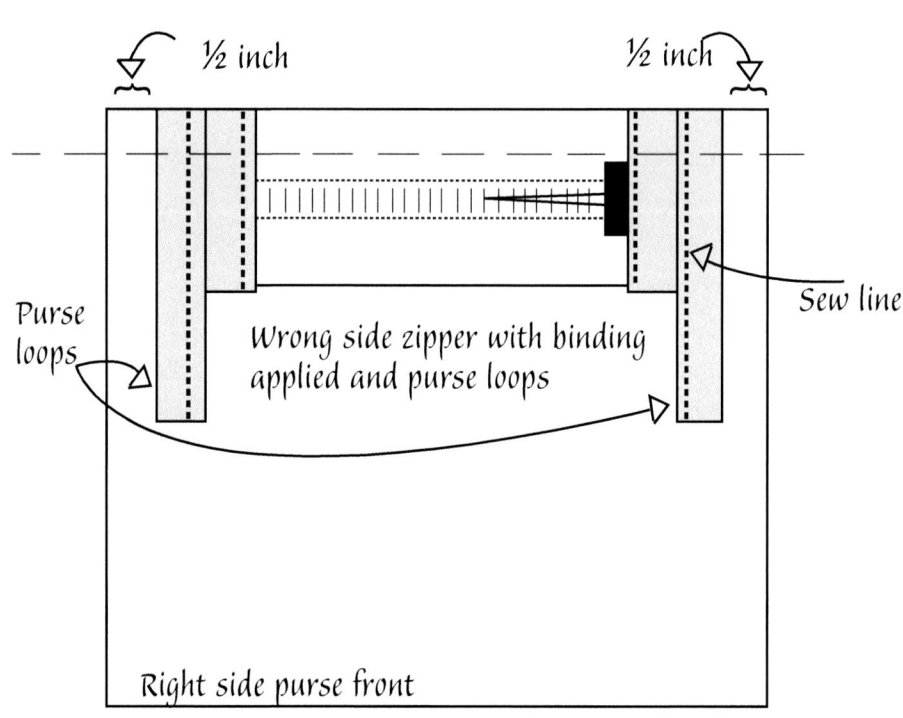

ABOVE: *Zipper in place face down at top of purse front and ready to be attached. This purse has purse loops.*

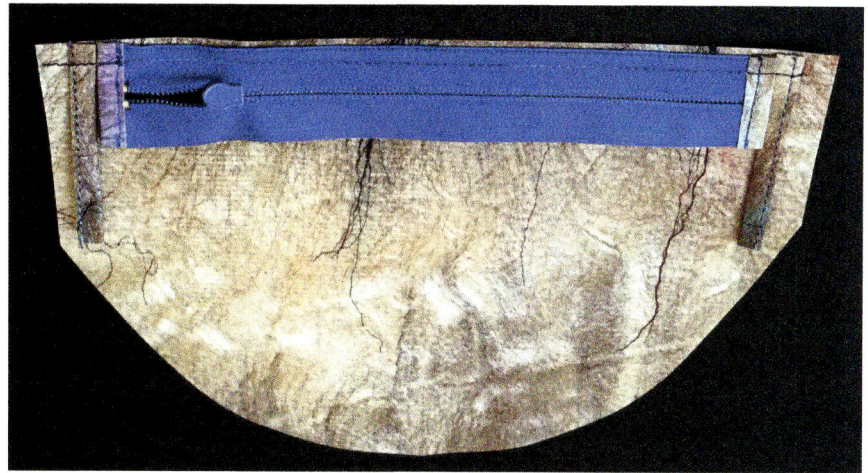

sew alongside the zipper pull because it is large and bulky. Before beginning to sew, open the zipper at least half way and sew along the zipper right up to the zipper pull. Then, with your needle in the down position, lift the machine presser foot, and move the zipper pull past the presser foot and into the fully open position. Continue sewing along the zipper and over the loop piece.

9. Press open, folding both the silk fusion edge and the zipper edge toward the back of the silk fusion piece. Top stitch on the right side a scant 1/8 inch from the folded edge, securing all edges neatly.

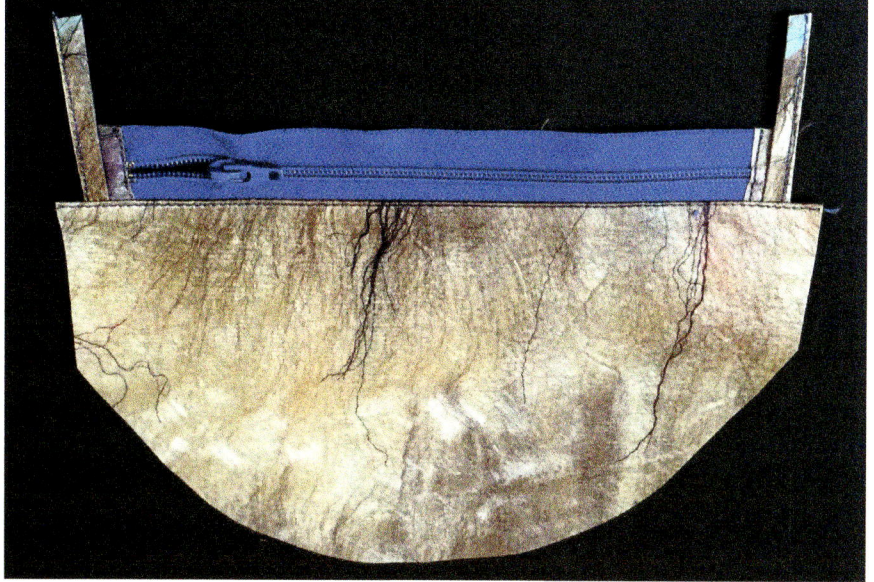

10. Sew the zipper to the other purse piece using the process described in step 8. Be careful to place the raw edges of the loops even with the raw edge of the top of the purse, with the loop (now it is a loop) toward the inside of the purse.

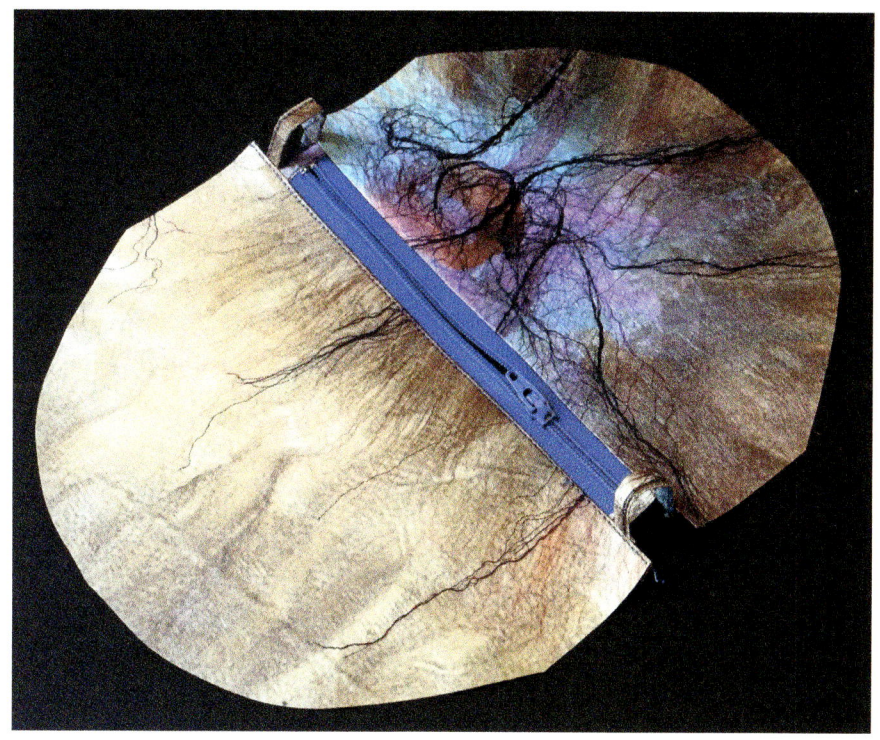

TOP: *The zipper is sewn in place between purse loops on the right side of the purse piece.* MIDDLE: *After the zipper is pressed to the wrong side of the purse piece, the fold is top-stitched.* RIGHT: *The zipper is sewn to both front and back pieces.*

SILK FUSION

11. Open the zipper all the way to allow the bag to be turned right side out. Align the two purse pieces right sides together, being careful to match the edges at the top of the purse. Sew the sides and bottom together with a ¼-inch seam. Be careful to keep the loops on the inside of the purse away from the side seam allowances.

12. Turn the purse right side out through the open zipper. Add a decorative handle or purse strap hardware. I like to tie a bit of yarn to the loop of the zipper pull, because the zipper pulls are often quite small and hard to grasp.

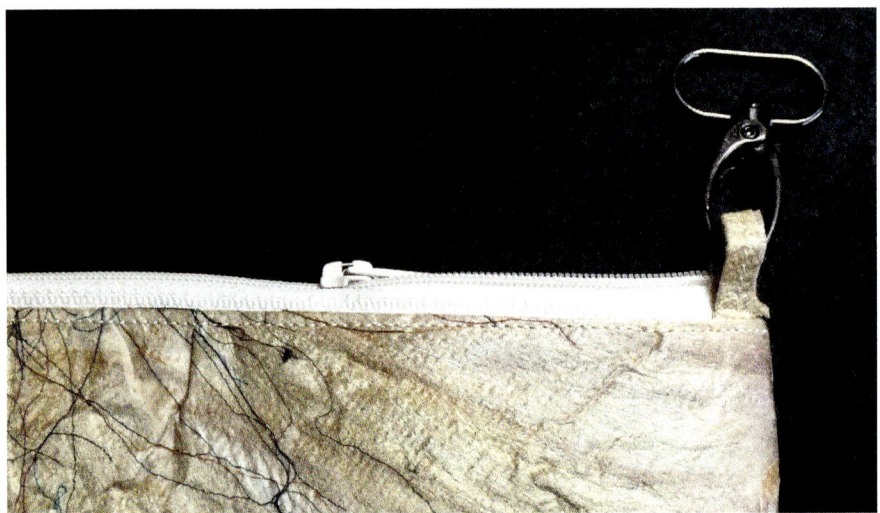

TOP: *Purse loops make it easy to attach hardware like this swivel clasp to be used with a strap.* RIGHT: *This petite silk fusion purse was designed to have a more rectangular shape.*

Lined Purse

SUPPLIES
Rotary cutter and mat or scissors
Ruler
Sewing machine
Basic sewing supplies

MATERIALS
Silk fusion in size necessary for your purse dimensions.

Fabric for lining in size necessary for your purse dimensions

Batting or felt in size necessary for your purse dimensions

Zipper in length necessary for your purse dimensions

Matching thread

Your choice of beads, buttons, embroidery floss or other embellishment

Purse strap made of chain, fabric or crocheted with yarn, in your desired length

ABOVE: *Colorful silk fusion shines in this purse.* BELOW: *Inside, a separator made of lining fabric divides the interior of the purse into two compartments and includes a handy pocket.*

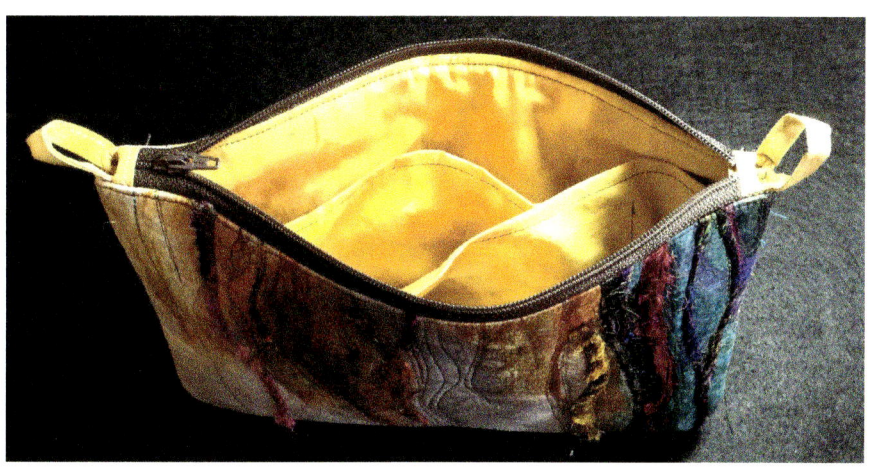

1. Draw a pattern or choose dimensions for your purse front and back. You can use two rectangular pieces, two squares, or you can add a curve to the sides or the bottom. The front and back pieces should be equal in size and shape.

2. Add any embellishments, such as stitching or beading, before construction of the purse begins. I like to add quilt stitching to my silk fusion purse pieces with one layer of batting or felt under the silk fusion. No backing fabric is needed for the quilting process because this purse is lined.

3. Cut your finished piece into two equal pieces. If you are using batting and have not quilted all the way to the edges, sew around all edges to secure batting to silk fusion.

4. Choose a lining fabric. When choosing a coordinating lining fabric, try to stay away from very dark fabric. If the lining is dark, it will be hard to see inside the purse and locate those little items that find their way to the bottom of our bags.

Cut two pieces of lining fabric about one inch larger on all sides than each of the purse pieces. If you want a separator

TOP AND ABOVE: *One piece of silk fusion is cut in half to form a purse front and back, then placed on lining pieces that are slightly larger than the purse front and back.*

piece in the purse, cut another piece of lining fabric twice as big your purse piece, as it will be folded in half. Additionally, if you want a pocket, cut a piece of fabric twice as big as the desired finished size of the pocket, as it will also be folded in half. You will also need a coordinating 1-by-8-inch strip of fabric for zipper binding and purse loops.

5. To create a binding piece for both ends of the zipper, fold the 1-by-8-inch strip in half lengthwise, wrong sides together and press. Now fold both edges into the pressed center and press again. You should have a strip that is four layers thick and only ¼-inch wide with no raw edges on top and bottom. Cut two 1-inch pieces from

SILK FUSION

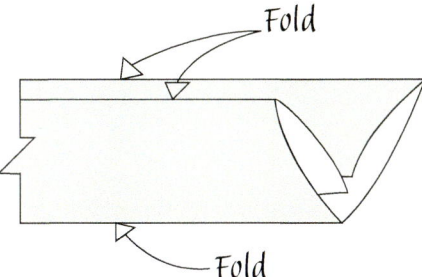

ABOVE: *To create the zipper binding, fold the fabric strip in half wrong sides together, then fold the edges into the center fold.*

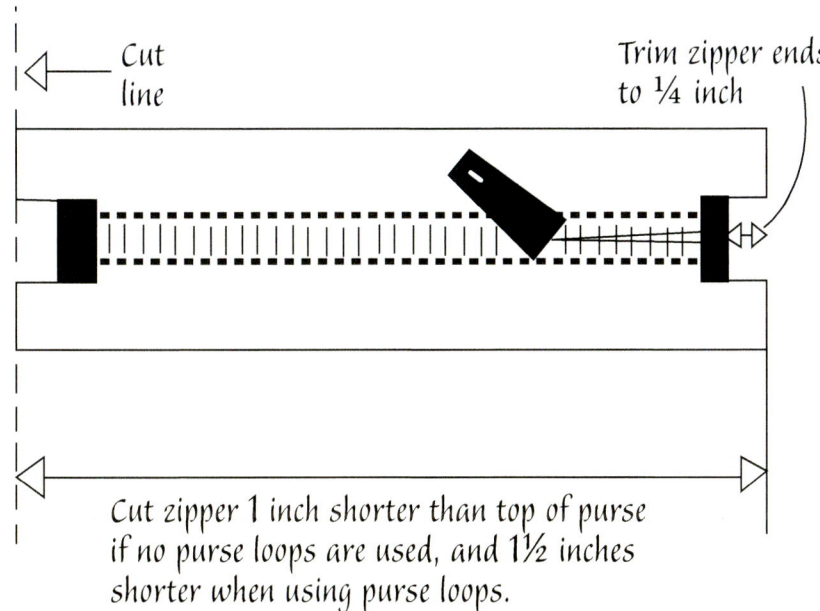

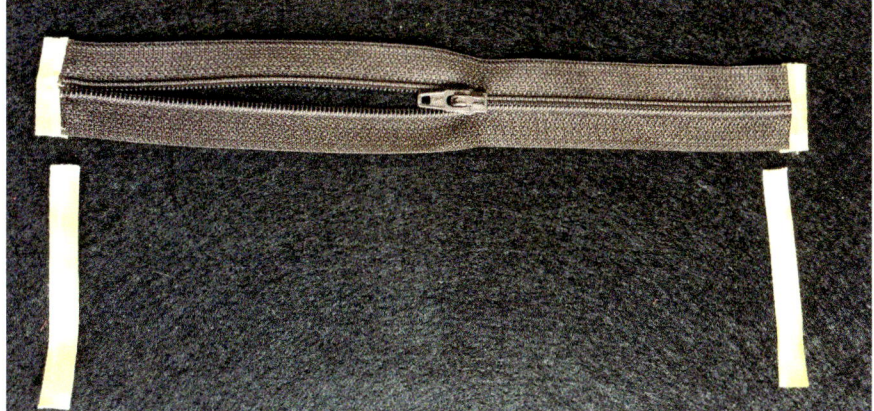

ABOVE: *Using lining fabric or another coordinating fabric, cut a strip to use for zipper binding and purse loops.*

the strip.

6. To prepare zipper, first trim the top edges of the zipper tape, leaving ¼ inch of the zipper ends from the first teeth. Then cut the zipper on the opposite end 1 inch shorter than the length of the top of the purse. When adding purse loops, the zipper should be cut 1½ inches shorter than the length of the top of the purse. If necessary, cut the end of the zipper right through the teeth (with utility scissors).

7. Unzip the zipper a few inches and machine stitch across the tape to hold the two halves together near the zipper stops. Now, slide the top end of the zipper into the fold of one of the 1-inch pieces of binding strip and sew the open edges of the binding strip together, catching the zipper between. Attach the other 1-inch binding piece to the other end of the zipper in the same fashion. (Your sewing machine will sew right through the teeth; but sew slowly.)

8. Cut the remaining binding strip into two 1½-inch pieces to be used as loops on the purse.

9. You will now sew the zipper into the lining and the quilted silk fusion piece. I do this in two stages, rather than pinning and

SILK FUSION

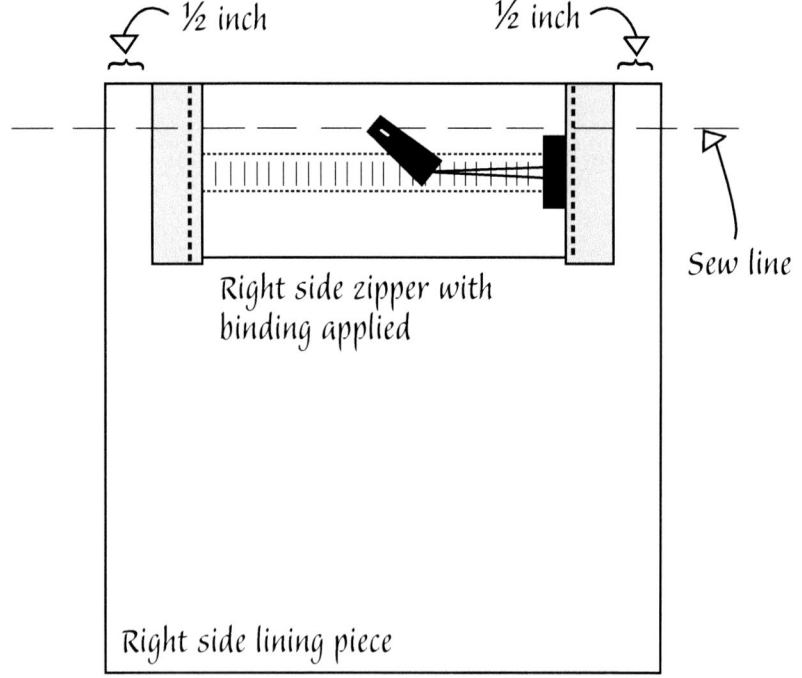

ABOVE: *Zipper in place face down at top of purse lining and ready to be attached. This purse does not include purse loops.*

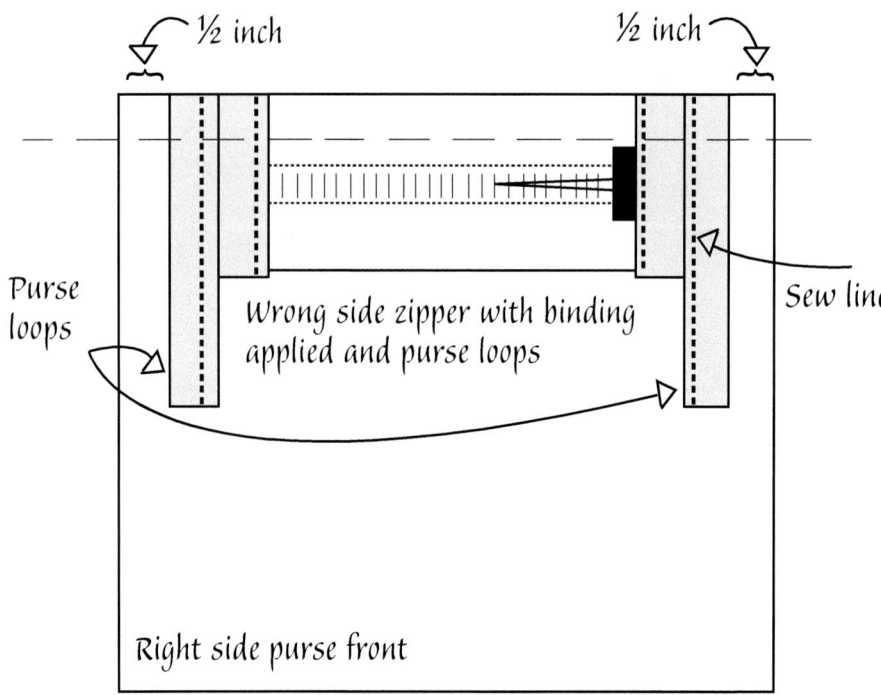

ABOVE: *Zipper in place face down at top of purse front and ready to be attached. This purse has purse loops.*

sewing all three layers together.

First, sew the zipper (and optional loops) to the lining fabric, with right sides of lining to back of zipper (with zipper pull facing up when laying on top of lining fabric). Position the zipper in the middle of the top of the lining piece and then place the two 1½-inch loop pieces (if you are including loops) to either side. Position the loop pieces with the length of loop lying toward the inside of the purse.

You should have at least ½ inch of lining fabric remaining along the outside of the purse loops or the zipper if no loops are included. Sew the zipper and loops to the top edge of the lining piece with a ¼-inch seam.

10. With most zippers, it is hard to sew alongside the zipper pull because it is large and bulky. Before beginning to sew, open the zipper at least half way and sew along the zipper right up to the zipper pull. Then, with your needle in the down position, lift the machine presser foot, and move the zipper pull past the presser foot and into the open position.

Continue sewing the zipper and second loop piece to the lining.

11. Now attach the zipper/loop/lining, as sewn (and not opened and pressed) to the quilted silk fusion

purse piece. Place the top of one purse piece, right side down to the right side of zipper on the zipper/loop/lining piece. Sew the silk fusion piece to the lining piece and zipper with a ¼-inch seam. Move the zipper head out of the way as in step 10.

12. Press all layers **away** from the zipper. Press well and then topstitch on the silk fusion piece a scant ⅛ inch away from the zipper/fold, catching the fold of the lining on the back. This topstitching will hold all the pieces nice and tight and leave you with a neat, finished look.

13. To attach the zipper to the other side of the purse, repeat steps 9, 10, 11 and 12 for both the lining and silk fusion pieces.

14. If you haven't already done so, sew remaining side and bottom edges of lining to silk fusion and trim excess lining even with silk fusion pieces.

15. Separator pieces and pockets are especially nice for larger purses. For the separator, use a piece of fabric that when folded in half is the same size as the purse pieces. Fold the separator piece in half, wrong sides together and sew ¼ inch from fold to give some stability to the separator piece.

ABOVE: *Zipper attached to purse front and lining and ready to be attached to purse back and lining. The yellow lining piece will need to be trimmed to match the purse front before the side seams are sewn.*

For the pocket, use a piece of fabric that when folded in half is the size you want for the pocket. Fold in half, right sides together and sew two sides closed with ¼-inch seams. Turn right side out, press and topstitch ¼-inch from fold for reinforcement.

16. Position the pocket on the separator piece where you want it to be with the raw edge of the pocket piece at the bottom.

17. Flip the pocket so it is upside down on the separator piece. Sew bottom of pocket to separator piece where shown using a ¼-inch seam.

18. Now flip the pocket back up into position and topstitch the sides in place through both layers of the purse separator.

19. You may like to finish the edges of the purse with a zigzag or serger before sewing the purse pieces together. Before you begin sewing all pieces of the purse together, open the zipper as far as it will go. This is very important because you will be turning the piece right side out through the zipper. Fold the purse in half at the zipper with the right sides of the silk fusion together, being careful to match the edges at the top of the purse. Also be careful to place the loops to the inside of the sandwich and away from the seam allowances. Place the separator piece on top of the layered pieces. Sew side and bottom edges through all layers: lined purse pieces and folded separator piece.

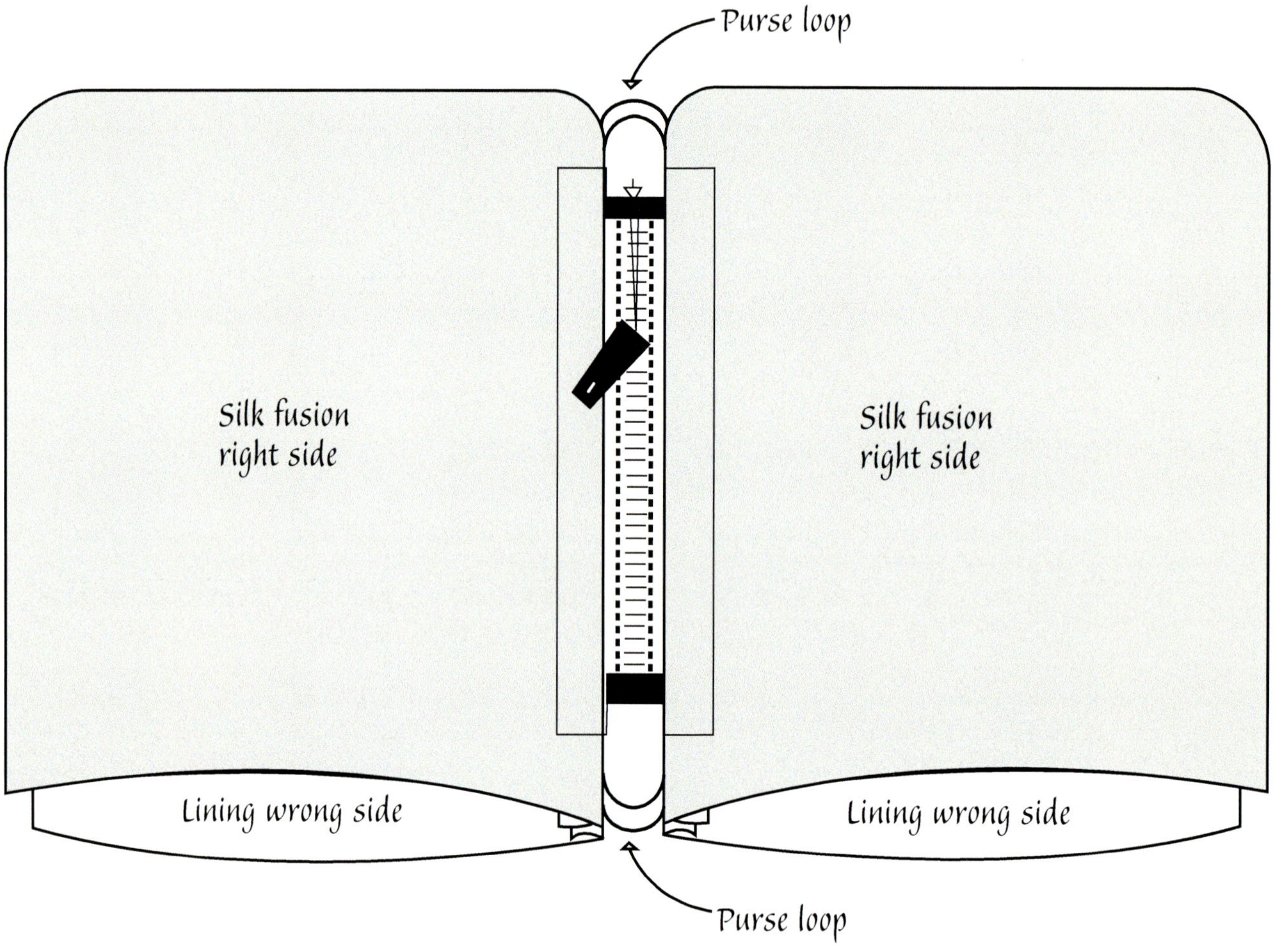

20. Turn right side out through the open zipper. Add decorative handle or purse strap hardware. I like to tie a bit of yarn to the loop on the zipper pull, because the zipper pulls are often quite small and hard to grasp.

ABOVE: *The zipper is sewn to the purse front, back and lining pieces and top stitched. Once the lining is trimmed, the side and bottom seams can be sewn.*

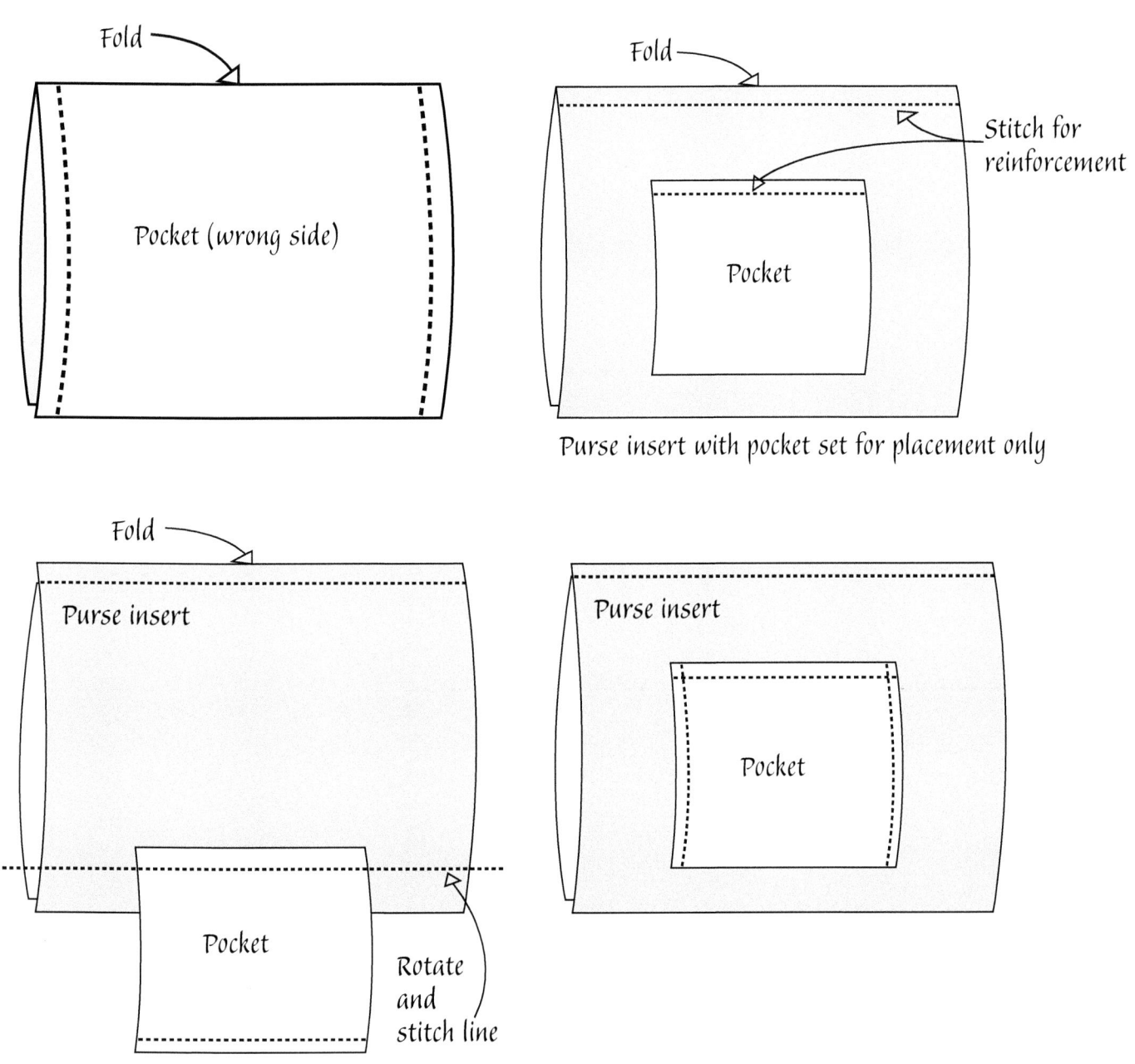

TOP LEFT: *To make the pocket, first fold the pocket piece in half, right sides together. Stitch along both sides, then turn right side out. Topstitch along folded edge of pocket.* TOP RIGHT: *Position pocket where you would like it located on the separator insert.* ABOVE LEFT: *Flip the pocket down, stitch along the bottom edge with a ¼-inch seam.* ABOVE RIGHT: *Flip the pocket up and secure with top-stitching along each side.*

SILK FUSION

Gallery

FLOW
18 by 18 in.
One piece of silk fusion, cut to reveal felt backing

All gallery artwork is by Tamara Leberer

BREAKING THROUGH

20 x 30 in.

Silk fusion and Angelina, machine quilted to cotton/batting backing. This is the first mosaic the author created.

SILK FUSION

OPPOSITE: **SILK SQUARED**

36 x 25 in.

Silk fusion squares machine stitched to background. Bits of silk sari ribbon, silk chiffon and Angelina fibers visible in background.

ABOVE: **SILK SQUARED** detail

SILK CITY
46 x 12 in.
Silk fusion layered with silk chiffon, machine stitched and hand stitched with pearl cotton. The "houses" are hand stitched, nuno-felted pieces.

ABOVE: **SILK CITY** detail

SILO
46 x 12 in.
Layered silk fusion, machine stitched to background

ABOVE: **SILO** detail

SILK FUSION

BAMBOO

28 x 50 in

Silk fusion and hand-dyed fabric, pieced and machine quilted

RIGHT AND FAR RIGHT: **BAMBOO** detail

SILK FUSION

SHAMEN
25 x 20 in.
Silk fusion and Angelina on cotton background. Machine quilted with Pellon as middle layer.

BLUE SQUARES
17 x 15 in.
Silk fusion squares machine stitched to background. Bits of silk sari ribbon, silk chiffon and Angelina fibers visible in background.

GOLD SQUARES
Each piece is 10 x 10 in.
Silk fusion squares machine stitched to background

SILK FUSION

POPPIES
24 x 18 in.
Silk fusion poppies and stems appliqued to silk fusion background, machine stitched. This was the author's first silk fusion art piece.

LEFT: **POPPIES** detail

Resources

SUPPLIES:

Atkinson Designs
www.atkinsondesigns.com
763-441-1825
Books, patterns and notions

Dharma Trading Co.
www.dharmatrading.com
800-542-5227
Angelina fibers

Dick Blick
www.dickblick.com
800-828-4548
Textile medium

Treenway Silks
The owner of Treenway Silks, Susan Du Bois, is truly passionate about her product, and I highly recommend her company. All the silk I use begins its journey in the capable hands of Treenway Silks.
www.treenwaysilks.com
888-383-7455
Silk tussah fibers, hankies, silk thread, textile medium

Treetops Colour Harmonies
www.treetopscolours.com
Tussah fibers, hankies, silk throwster waste, textile medium

REFERENCES:
Making Silk Fusion
by Sue Bleiweiss,
www.suebleiweiss.com/freeprojects/silk.pdf

TexereSilk Department
New England Mercantile Group, LLC
50 Inwood Road, Suite 6
Rocky Hill, CT 06067
History of silk production and silk industry

Treenway Silks
2060 Miller Court
Lakewood, CO 80215
History and biology of the silk worm

Wild Fibres
Studio I-135, The Custard Factory
Gibb St, Birmingham B9 4AA, UK
History, biology of the silk worm

Acknowledgements

I'd like to thank my incredible family and fantastic friends.

It is said that you can't choose your family. I consider myself one of the luckiest people on earth because my entire family is supportive and interested in my creative endeavors and just generally fun to be around. So I'd like to thank my family for their heart-felt support.

This statement also infers that you can choose your friends. So, friends of mine, thank you for choosing me! You are all so special, talented and kind: That is why I chose you!

Writing a book is truly a group effort, and I was guided through this process by a wonderful team, each member a creative genius. My editor, Janice Brewster, and designer, Karen Sulmonetti, masterfully transformed an abundance of text and a menagerie of photographs into a book that I will treasure for my lifetime. Along the way I have gathered many bits of wisdom from some very special people: Carol Ann Waugh, Katie Fowler and Mike Daniels.

Of course, I always learn the most from my talented students!

I'm sure I will meet many more praiseworthy individuals before this process is complete. My deep appreciation goes out to all!

And for keeping me company while I toiled away in the studio, patiently waiting for his walk; my precious, giant, shadow dog, Cooper.

About the Author

Tamara Leberer has taught silk fusion, along with many other fiber art techniques such as felting, nuno felting, modern quilt piecing and free motion quilting, in Colorado since 2011.

As an artist, Tamara is driven by creating beauty, first and foremost. She prefers to create what she, personally, feels is appealing. Her inspiration comes from the colors of nature, the built environment and the classic definitions of design. Still, she is a rule-breaking, get-it-done kind of gal.

Trying new things, always trying new things, and putting things together in new ways fuels Tamara's creativity. Her ideas come from a conglomeration of traditional and aesthetic skills picked up through her personal and professional life in architecture, sewing and gardening.

Whether you call them art quilts or fiber art, Tamara's work revolves around a love of fiber, fabric and color. She finds the vivid colors of fiber and fabric and the texture and dimensionality of quilting thrilling. No matter what or how much she does, she can't extinguish her passion to create with her hands. Her favorite manner of work is improvisational, where she explores line, shape and color to create harmony and motion.

Tamara has spent the last 15 years exploring every facet of fiber art before finding the sweet spot that makes her artist heart feel at home: combining a wide variety of fibers in different ways, and then quilting, always quilting.

"As my artist statement explains,
my work is utterly incomprehensible
and is therefore full of deep significance."
– *Calvin and Hobbes*

© Copyright 2015 Tamara B. Leberer
ALL RIGHTS RESERVED
No part of this book may be reproduced in any manner without the express written consent of the author except in the case of brief excerpts in critical reviews and articles. All inquiries should be addressed to the contact information listed on this website: www.creativegirlfriendspress.com

ISBN: 978-0-9884282-2-5

Creative Girlfriends Press
103 Wentworth Ave.
Cincinnati, Ohio 45215

Developmental Editor: Janice Brewster, www.creativegirlfriendspress.com
Design Director: Karen Sulmonetti, www.sulmonettidesign.com
Photography by Wes Magyar (pages 4, 33, 74-81, 83 and 84), Thom Harrop (pages 6, 34, 37, 46, 47 and 85) and Tamara Leberer. Stock photo page 9, alamy.com

SILK *Fusion*

Lush color for fiber art, quilts and mixed media

Tamara B. Leberer